HAUNTED LANDSCAPES

VOLUME ONE

SHUCKLAND

Weird tales, ghosts, folklore and legends

from East Anglia's Waveney valley

CHARLES CHRISTIAN

Heart of Albion

Charles Christian is an English barrister and Reuters correspondent turned writer, award-winning tech journalist, and podcaster with a soft spot for history: one side of his family came over with the Vikings, while the other is best remembered for some unpleasantness aboard *HMS Bounty*.

He writes and presents the weekly *Weird Tales Radio Show* podcast, which looks at folklore, urban myths, ghost stories, geek culture and the paranormal, as well as running the *Weird Tales Video Show* YouTube channel. He is a regular contributor on folklore and medieval history to the *Ancient Origins* online community. And a national newspaper once sent him on a werewolf hunt – in Hull. Spoiler alert: he didn't find one.

Born a 'chime child' with a caul so, according to legend, he cannot drown at sea but can see and talk to ghosts and fairy folk without fear of coming to harm – superpowers he didn't need to employ while writing this book.

Join us on a journey exploring the weird wonders of the Waveney valley.

Behind the ruined castles, soaring church towers and attractive market towns lie ancient legends and folklore.

Ghosts of avenging kings, highwaymen, headless queens, ancient buried treasures, demonic entities, notorious villains, treacherous barons, murderous earls, ley-lines, paganism, yew-shrouded churchyards, old ivy-covered houses, witchcraft, strange fearsome beasts – including the notorious Black Shuck who gives his name to *Shuckland.*

Shuckland
Weird tales, ghosts, folklore and legends
from East Anglia's Waveney valley

Charles Christian

Volume One in the Haunted Landscapes series

Cover illustration: the ruins of St Mary's church, Thorpe Parva.

ISBN 978-1-905646-35-7

Published by
Heart of Albion
8 Hedgefield Road, Barrowby
Grantham, NG32 1TA
albion@indigogroup.co.uk

Visit our Web site: www.hoap.co.uk

Printed in England by Imprint Academic Ltd

DEDICATION

To Janie. Your love, support, encouragement and enthusiasm put the ink on my typewriter ribbon and the words into my wordprocessor. You also curb my natural tendency to begin every second sentence with 'however'.

CONTENTS

FOREWORD

I consider myself reasonably familiar with the Waveney valley, as I live only fifteen or so miles away to the north. Over the past few years I've frequently passed through that landscape of attractive villages, agricultural fields and flood meadows en route to the Suffolk coast, and spent time wandering around the fascinating old market towns of Diss, Harleston, Bungay and Beccles. I'd like to think I'm moderately acquainted with some of its history and folklore – but reading Charles Christian's excellent *Shuckland*, I soon come to realise that my own comprehension of the area is that of an occasional visitor, and only skims the surface of strange characters, historical coincidences and weird supernatural goings-on that sit beneath the area's genteel façade of medieval churches and bucolic peacefulness; originally from Yorkshire, Charles has now lived half of his life in the Waveney valley, and his knowledge of the place shows.

Yet contained among the nuggets of local lore are a number of archetypal stories that resonate in other parts of the East Anglian countryside – and elsewhere in the British Isles; reading *Shuckland*, brought to mind many similar tales – and linked historical figures – found in my own adopted south Norfolk, as well as further to the west in the area around Swaffham where my grandmother lived, and the Lincolnshire Fens where I grew up. Turning its pages was something of a trip into memory, reminding me of the tale of the Mistletoe Bride, which I borrowed and used in my first novel *The Listeners*: the now-defunct Brockdish Old Hall on the Waveney's north bank is said to be a potential location for the story, along with three others in Somerset and Hampshire.

More prosaically, Charles's book summoned up a meeting with Ditchingham's famous chicken man, Gordon Knowles (a lovely old boy, I recall), some twenty years ago; I was there as part of an Anglian Television crew which was filming his daily ritual of feeding his flock, before taking his constitutional swim in the Waveney. How long, I wonder, will his traffic island on the A143 continue to be known as the Chicken Roundabout; will it persist beyond the memories of those ageing drivers who actually witnessed him chucking corn to the hungry hens? Even now, do early-morning walkers once in a while spot a pale form splashing through those dark waters as they round one of the river's gentle bends...

So, relax and enjoy *Shuckland*. Whether you're from the area and already know the bare bones of some of these stories or, like me, are a visitor from further afield, it doesn't matter. Charles has a great overview of history and knows how to spin a good yarn: you are in skilled hands.

Edward Parnell

Author of *Ghostland: In Search of a Haunted Country* (HarperCollins, 2019)

PROLOGUE

WAVENEY - A LIMINAL PLACE

East Anglia is a liminal place, midway between the land and the sea, the earth and the sky, the present day and one thousand, thousand years of history. Flint, sand, clay, clunch and carstone edging against brooks, rivers, meres, broads, estuaries and the ocean. And big skies pierced only by medieval towers – this is where England began.

Although not Norfolk born-and-bred, I've now lived and worked in the Waveney valley for half my life. It's the place I call home and for all its foibles (don't get me started on the woeful broadband and lack of mains drainage) I love it. The countryside is gorgeous. The skies are spectacular, especially at sunrise and sunset. And the roads are generally so free of traffic, it's like driving in the 1950s. Actually better than the 1950s as cars today are so much more safe, reliable and comfortable.

The Waveney valley is also full of history. Along with the ruined castles, soaring church towers and attractive market towns, there are so many legends and so much folklore – some ancient, some relatively modern – as to give the place an air of intriguing weirdness.

Old traditions, ghosts of avenging kings, highwaymen, headless queens, ancient buried treasures, demonic entities, notorious villains, treacherous barons, murderous earls, ley-lines, paganism, yew-shrouded churchyards, old ivy-covered houses, witchcraft, strange fearsome beasts – including the notorious Black Shuck who gives his name to *Shuckland* – and frequently involve incidents uniquely linked to the landscape. In many ways the Waveney valley's vibe echoes the current enthusiasm for Earth mysteries, psychogeography, Gothic tourism, and folk horror.

For my own part, this is meat and drink for me. I've always been a fan of reading about and hunting for 'ghoulies and ghosties. And long-leggety beasties. And things that go bump in the night' since growing up in a spooky old house, down by the harbour-side in Scarborough.

My research into the folklore, ghosts and legends of the Waveney valley has also confirmed my belief that truth really is often stranger than fiction. And that no matter how far-fetched a tale may seem, if you dig down beneath the surface, you will discover a factual basis for the story.

Let me explain the organisation of this book... Part One is a gazetteer of the Waveney valley, guiding you from the river's source and down to the sea. This is a route, as I explain later, that coincides with the path of a significant ley-line but don't worry, most of the time I use the ley-line as a framing device.

In Part Two, I deep dive into the mysteries surrounding the Old Minster ruins at South Elmham and how they tie in with the ley-line – and also ancient trackways and trade routes, including the Icknield Way.

And, in the Appendix, I provide some background information to people and events mentioned in Parts One and Two or else because some of the material I researched was just too weird not to include in this book. You'll also find a few "Quite Intriguing Too's" dotted throughout the main narrative.

One final point: do I personally believe in ghosts, the weird and the paranormal? My answer is the same as the ghost and supernatural horror writer M.R. James gave to the same question in the preface to a new collection of his stories about a hundred years ago: 'I am prepared to consider the evidence and accept it if it satisfies me.'

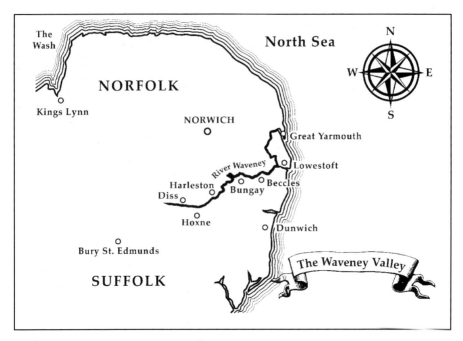

The Waveney Valley today.

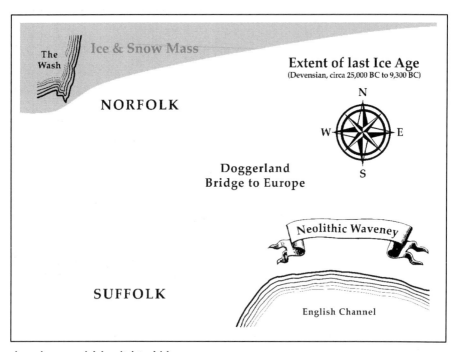

Ice Age and Neolithic Waveney.

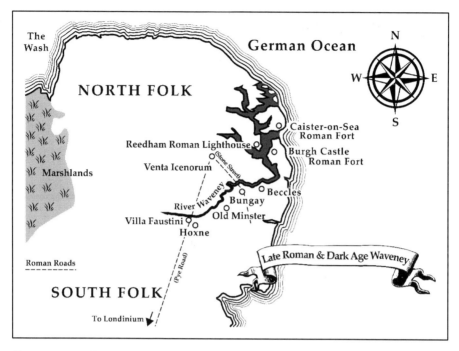

Roman and Dark Age Waveney.

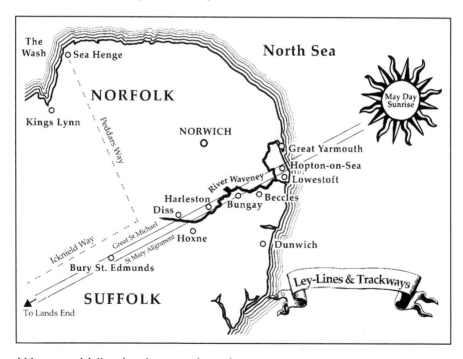

Waveney Valley ley-lines and trackways.

PART ONE: GAZETTEER

ALL ALONG THE WAVENEY

Chapter 1

Treachery at the Abbey

It is May 25th in the year 1067, and a Saxon abbot is screaming for mercy at the end of a Norman noose as he is hanged from the gatehouse of his own abbey. Welcome to the Waveney valley, a sleepy fold in the landscape in England's rural East Anglia.

Who was this unfortunate abbot? Why did he meet such an untimely end? Let's turn back the clock a few weeks to earlier in the spring of that year...

Although William of Normandy (better known as William the Conqueror) had been crowned King of England on Christmas Day 1066, many parts of England were still resisting Norman rule. This included East Anglia, where one of the leading churchmen, Ethelwold (or Aelfwald), the abbot of St Benet's, had been put in command of the naval and military defence of the East Coast by Harold Godwinson, the last Saxon king of England.

By the early spring of 1067, King Harold had been dead six months (killed by the arrow that hit him in the eye during the Battle of Hastings) leaving Ethelwold and his followers holed up in the isolated but seemingly impregnable island fortress of St Benet's Abbey, in what is now the carefully tended Norfolk Broads but was then just a maze of rivers, meres, wide tidal estuaries, mud banks and salt marshes accessible only by boat or across a long narrow causeway from Horning.

With all previous frontal assaults on the abbey having failed, William, the new Norman king, now put young Roger Bigod in charge of capturing St Benet's.

The Medieval gatehouse and later Georgian mill tower, St Benet's Abbey. Photo: Charles Christian.

Until a few years previously, the Bigods (or *le Bigots* as the family name was originally spelled) had been a family of poor and relatively obscure knights from Calvados in Normandy. One source describes Roger, born in around 1040, as a hearth-knight in the service of William's half-brother Odo, the Bishop of Bayeux. The term hearth-knight derives from knights who were landless and lived in the castle or fortress of a local noble. At night they would sleep on the floor of the castle's great hall but their status allowed them a place by the hearth, close to the fire, where it would be warmer.

Despite these lowly origins, the Bigods had earned themselves a reputation as useful people to have around, having earlier alerted William to a conspiracy against him and, later, sailing with the invasion fleet to fight at Hastings. Today we'd call Roger a chancer, a man rose to become one of William's enforcers – the people you'd call in when there was dirty work to be done quick – although in the light of their history over the next 250 years, perhaps a better way to visualise the Bigods would be as the bosses of an old-style Chicago mafia crime family.

Recognising the strength of Abbot Ethelwold's position at St Benet's, Roger Bigod changed tack and opened negotiations to end the siege without further violence. Ethelwold for hs part saw that while the Normans could not get into the abbey, neither he nor his Saxons could get out and so, playing for time, he agreed to a truce and appointed a respected and long serving monk called Brother Essric as his intermediary.

Essric (some accounts say his name was Veritas) may have served the abbey loyally for over twenty years but Bigod was a better judge of character than Abbot Ethelwold and was able to detect Brother Essric was an unhappy man. A man seething with resentment because he felt he had been overlooked for higher office and was now caught up in a life or death struggle brought on by his own abbot's dabbling in politics. It was at this point in the negotiations that Bigod made Essric an offer he could not refuse.

If Essric would open the abbey gates to the Normans in the middle of the night, then – so the legend runs – not only would Bigod spare the lives of all the monks but he would also make Essric the new abbot 'for life' and 'raise him higher than any man living within the abbey… higher than he would ever expect from a friend'.

The deal was struck. Essric agreed to betray the abbey to his new friend during matins, which during the late spring a medieval monastic order would have celebrated at around three in the morning. The gate was opened, the Normans rushed in, the guards dozing in the gatehouse were overcome, and the abbey was seized.

Then it was time for Brother Essric to receive his just rewards from Roger Bigod. First an abbot's highly decorated cope (in effect a cape) was placed over his shoulders. Then the mitre (ceremonial headdress) was placed on his head then a crosier (ceremonial staff of office) thrust into his right hand. But Bigod had one further reward in store for the newly-appointed abbot and that was to slip a rope noose over his head.

To Essric's horror, the other end of the rope had already been hung over the highest point of the gatehouse and, at Bigod's signal, the Normans began hauling on it, raising Essric 'higher than any man living within the abbey'.

The Normans may have liked to get their own way and were ruthless in the methods they used to achieve this but they also didn't like traitors, no matter whose side they betrayed.

That was the short unhappy career of Abbot Essric although it is claimed that on the anniversary of his treachery, his screams can still be heard and his ghost seen hanging by a noose from the ruined, but now distinctly picturesque, abbey gatehouse.

As for Roger Bigod? Over the next few years he and his family would emerge as the dominant military and political force in this part of East Anglia.

So welcome to the Waveney valley. It is a place where weirdness, tradition and strangeness prevails – yet also, as we shall see, a place where decisive moments in English history have taken place and where never adequately explained mysteries linger to this day.

QUITE INTRIGUING TOO

The Ghost of Brother Essric

People taking boating holidays on the Norfolk Broads still moor up around the ruins of St Benet's Abbey on May 25th in the hope of seeing the ghostly execution of Brother Essric although the last reported sighting I can find any reference to occurred before the First World War. Perhaps this was an example of what is known as a 'residual haunting' where, like an over-played recording on video tape, the ghostly manifestation has become worn out with age and will never be seen again.

QUITE
INTRIGUING
TOO

Residual Hauntings

Residual or imprint hauntings are the most frequent type of ghost sighting, where the apparition is oblivious to its surroundings, and anyone present, and just keeps living out the same set of past events over and over again. You can't communicate with this type of ghost. In fact there is a suggestion, known as the *The Stone Tape* theory (after the 1972 BBC TV play of the same name), that they are not so much spectral beings but a playback, like a video, of an event in the ghost's past life that was so powerfully emotional it left an imprint or recording in the surrounding fabric of a building or landscape. That's why you frequently hear reports of ghost sightings at the scenes of murders, executions, fatal accidents and battles.

CHAPTER 2

WHERE THE WAVENEY VALLEY IS NOW
– AND WHERE IT WAS ONCE

To make sense of some aspects of the history and legends of the Waveney valley, it helps to know not only where it is today but also where was it in historical times. For example there are accounts of Viking longships sailing past the town of Bungay and upstream to Diss yet in recent years this section of the river has become little more than a stream that cannot be navigated even by canoe.

Let's start with the basics. We are talking about East Anglia on the east coast of England, where the River Waveney forms the boundary between the counties of Norfolk and Suffolk, flowing for a total of 58 miles before it reaches the coast at approximately the most easterly point of the United Kingdom. It flows past the historic market towns of Diss, Harleston, Bungay, and Beccles. Then, after Beccles, the route of the River Waveney leaves the surrounds of its valley and enters a wide, flat area of marshland, becoming part of the Norfolk Broads before flowing out into the North Sea.

It has been suggested the name Waveney is derived from 'waving waters' because the river was filled with reeds that waved in the breeze. Which is nicely picturesque. Sadly the true origin of the name is the rather less romantic Old English *wagen*, meaning quagmire and *ça*, meaning running water, stream or river – in other word: a river running through a marsh. The first written reference to the *Wahenhe* dates back to the twelfth century.

Given the origins of its name, it is perhaps appropriate our story starts in an unprepossessing ditch on the east side of the B1113 road, about six miles to the west of Diss between the villages of Redgrave in Suffolk and South Lopham in Norfolk. This is the source of the River Waveney.

Curiously, the ditch on the other side of the road is the source of the River Little Ouse which continues the county boundary west, via the Great Ouse, until it reaches the sea at King's Lynn. It could be argued the great canal builders of the Industrial Revolution missed an opportunity here to link the two rivers and create a continuous inland waterway between the East Coast and the Wash. Still, at times of heavy rainfall, when both ditches flood, Norfolk technically does become an island separated from the rest on the UK. In fact this 'island' of Norfolk constitutes the largest of the United Kingdom's many islands – for example it is ten times the size of the Isle of Man.

From this inauspicious start, the Waveney runs into what is now the Redgrave and Lopham Fen, which is both a Site of Special Scientific Interest (SSSI) and a Ramsar site – one of a number of important wetlands around the world run according to an international treaty agreed in the eponymous Iranian city in 1971. To the casual visitor, one of its most significant features is the herd of Polish Konik ponies, a primitive, semi-feral breed of horse that were imported to graze the wetter areas of the fen.

For scientists, especially arachnologists, the area's greatest claim to fame is it is the home of the first recorded UK population of the Great Raft Spider (or Fen Raft Spider, *Dolomedes plantarius*). In fact the local *Diss Express* newspaper once joked that the Redgrave and Lopham Fen had received so much money by way of national and international conservations grants, that the spiders had abandoned their rafts as they could now afford motor boats. But back to the river.

Just a couple of miles west of the source of the Waveney lies both Garboldisham Heath, where a lone Bronze Age round barrow is one of the many, many places claimed to be the final resting place of the legendary Queen Boudicca (or Boadicea), and Knettishall Heath, the location of the eastern end of the ancient Icknield Way long distance track. (More about trackways later in this book.)

To the south of the source is the village of Redgrave, where the church – one the many dedicated to St Mary we will encounter in this book – contains a spectacular memorial to Lord Chief Justice Holt, who died 1710. This judge is best known for doing much to stop the persecution of alleged witches through the English courts by introducing an element of long overdue unprejudiced scepticism into proceedings.

After the Redgrave and Lopham Fen, the Waveney runs along at the back of the Bressingham garden centre and railway museum, across Roydon Fen and into Diss where it continues its ditch-like appearance at the back of a supermarket car park, before starting to wind its way across the water meadows beyond Scole.

This next section of the river was once a hive of industrial activity, with the Waveney being used to power at least fifteen mills working everything from grinding corn and milling flour to driving the looms used to weave linen and drabbet (coarse cotton) cloth. The first mention of milling on the Waveney occurs in the *Domesday Book* in 1086 and the last mill ceased operation in 1968, almost nine centuries later. Many of the mill buildings are still standing, some retain their wheels and machinery, but most have been converted into homes.

As the river approaches Bungay, there are several large lakes that were once the Weybread gravel pits but are now used for fishing, while in recent years the Mendham Marshes area has been frequently and dramatically flooded. That said, for most of its part, this section of the river is too shallow to be navigated although canoes, rowing boats and other unpowered craft are permitted along some sections between Brockdish and Ellingham.

By far the most spectacular section here is the large oxbow bend around Outney Common (now home to the Bungay and Waveney Valley Golf Club) that passes beneath the Bath Hills. (Technically Bungay sits at the neck of a meander of the Waveney.) Back in 1670, an Act of Parliament was passed permitting a group of Bungay traders to carry out improvements to the River Waveney, including the construction of a staithe (a small wharf or quay) and a series of locks between the town and Beccles, where the river becomes tidal.

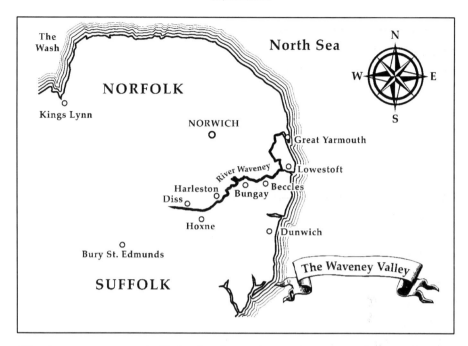

The investment paid off, for by the eighteenth century Bungay Staithe was the commercial heart of the town, with timber, cloth, malt, corn and dairy products produced in the Bungay area being sent by river to other large towns in the area, including Beccles, Lowestoft and Great Yarmouth, and from there by sea to London.

In return, the increasingly wealthy burghers, merchants and bankers of Bungay imported coal and, in 1754, a rather impressive stone statue of *Justice* that still stands on top of the Butter Cross in the market square. In fact Matthias Kerrison, who owned the staithe and the navigation rights in the late eighteenth century, made so much money from trade that he became the town's first millionaire.

Providing the river transport between Bungay and the rest of the Waveney valley (and also across the entire Norfolk network of rivers, meres and broads) were hundreds of flat-bottomed gaff-rigged sailing barges called wherries, that could each transport about twenty-five tons of cargo. Wherries traditionally had black sails as a result of being treated with a preservative mixture of tar and fish oil.

Sadly, by the mid-nineteenth century the railways were providing a cheaper and faster alternative to river transport between the

Waveney valley towns. Trade began to fall off at Bungay Staithe, with a result that less money was spent on river maintenance and it began to silt up. The end came in 1934 when navigation rights were removed from Bungay, and Geldeston Lock became the head (or end-point) of navigation.

The demise of the wherries was equally swift and, no longer commercially viable as a result of competition by first rail and later road transport, by the end of World War Two there were none left trading on the Norfolk Broads. After that, the vast majority were left to rot at their moorings or else deliberately sunk, in some instances to strengthen riverbanks, so that today there are just eight wherries left sailing on the Norfolk Broads.

From Geldeston, the Waveney wends its way down on to Beccles, where it becomes a far wider river more than capable of handling the large volumes of yachts and pleasure cruisers that now ply the Norfolk Broads during the summer holiday season.

Now let's complete our route by following it to the sea. You might assume the river would continue in its west-to-east direction, which would take it, via Oulton Broad, to the coast at Lowestoft but you'd be wrong. In fact shortly before Oulton the Waveney turns back on itself in a north-westerly direction for a few miles before twisting to the north-east to join the River Yare at the entrance to Breydon Water and then, finally, flowing into the North Sea at Great Yarmouth.

That said, thanks to river improvement works, there is a one mile stretch of water called the Oulton Dyke (originally dug in the eighteenth century and subsequently widened) that directly connects the Waveney to Oulton Broad, Lake Lothing and the sea at Lowestoft.

All this relates to the river as it is now but what of its past?

As already mentioned, in my references to Viking longships and the fact Bungay used to be a significant port, the River Waveney was once a far wider and impressive waterway than we see today. But how much so?

The old Roman fort of Gariannonum or Burgh Castle.
Photo: Charles Christian.

Let's wind back the clock seventeen centuries to the era when this part of the world still belonged to the Roman Empire's province of Britannia and the geography was entirely different. The town of Great Yarmouth did not exist yet and even its site was below sea level, with the waters of the Great Estuary flowing above it.

The Great Estuary was where the rivers Yare and Waveney, as well as the Chet, Tass, Bure and Ant, joined together before flowing into the North Sea. To the west was the market town of *Venta Icenorum* (the place of the Iceni) close to what is now the village of Caistor St Edmund, about five miles south of present-day Norwich.

What today is the Norfolk Broads town of Reedham was, in Roman times, a coastal village complete with its own lighthouse or, perhaps, watch-tower. Archaeological excavations have revealed the town's medieval church of St John the Baptist was constructed using the foundations, stone and brickwork from the earlier Roman building.

To the north-east, on an island, was the Roman fort of Caister-on-Sea, while the south-east was the massive Saxon Shore fort of *Gariannonum* – modern-day Burgh Castle. And to the south lay Beccles, then a coastal town that, by the eleventh century, would be famous for its herring fishing industry.

Wind back the clock back even further – not by seventeen but by over seventy centuries – to 7000 BC and the waters of the Great Estuary flowed into a tidal bay whose eastern boundary comprised the lowlands, marshes, lagoons, and islands of Doggerland – the last remnants of the land bridge that once connected the peninsular of Britain to the rest of continental Europe.

Today, the River Waveney may be a relatively little-known English river, less than sixty miles in length – and only navigable for half that distance – yet it is a waterway whose history stretches back beyond the Roman and Celtic eras and into prehistory and mythical times.

And did I mention that for much of its path, the Waveney valley coincides with the route of a ley-line. Not just any ley-line but the Great St Michael and St Mary Alignment (or 'corridor of incidence' or even 'geomantic corridor') that is probably the most famous ley-line in the country, if not the world. I'll be explaining more about ley-lines later in this book but until then, make a mental note of the number of churches we encounter dedicated to either the Archangel Michael or the Virgin Mary. Churches dedicated to St Mary can be found almost exclusively on the northern side of the valley, whereas the St Michael churches lie to the south of the River Waveney.

Geography lesson over, let's get on with the valley's folklore, ghosts, history and legends.

CHAPTER 3

DISS AND THE TWO SIDES OF A TOWN SIGN – THE JOURNEY BEGINS

Our starting point is the south Norfolk town of Diss. Unlike many rural market towns which suffered disastrous fires at some point during the sixteenth and seventeenth centuries – narrow lanes, old timber buildings, thatched roofs and open fires do not make a happy combination – Diss still retains a high proportion of Tudor and Elizabethan timber-framed buildings originating from the days when the town was a centre for the wool and weaving trades.

Without doubt Diss's most significant feature is the almost circular mere in the centre of the town. It covers an area of six acres (2.4 ha) and the water is up to 18 feet (6 m) deep with an estimate of at least another 50 feet (16 m) of mud and sediment below that. It has been claimed this makes the Mere the second-deepest lake in England. Unlike the Norfolk Broads, which are largely manmade arising from flooded medieval peat-workings, the Mere at Diss is clearly natural in origin. But what created it?

Suggestions include that it is a flooded impact crater from a prehistoric meteorite strike or the flooded caldera of an extinct volcano. Sadly, scientific research indicates a rather less dramatic explanation, namely it is a flooded sink-hole caused by the collapse of caves in the chalk bedrock at some point during the one of the Ice Ages between 450,000 and 130,000 years ago.

An alternative suggestion is the Mere is a collapsed pingo, a form of post-glacial depression. Also called kettle lakes (and, in a couple, of melodramatic instances 'shrieking pits' where there are associated ghost stories) there used to be hundreds of pingos in the Breckland area to the west of a Diss. Most have been obliterated by farming but there are still dozens to be seen on the Great Eastern Pingo trail near Thompson in Thetford Forest (about twenty miles north-west of Diss) but they are all far, far smaller than Diss Mere.

With the Mere lying on the St Michael/St Mary ley-line, this has also fueled a rumour that at the bottom of the Mere you will find one of the gates to the underworld. This stems from a suggestion the town takes its name from *Dis Pater*, the Roman god of the underworld, although a rather more prosaic explanation is it's derived from the Old English/Anglo-Saxon *Dic* (later spelled *Dize* and *Disce*), meaning standing water or a lake.

A Short History of Markets in Diss

The official histories of Diss market agree there was once a now long-lost royal charter dating back to 1185 and the reign of King Henry II. This granted a Norman baron by the name of Sir Walter Fitz-Robert, who was also Lord of the Manor of Diss, the right to hold a weekly market every Friday (which still takes place over 900 years later) and an annual autumn fair.

In 1295 Sir Walter's great-grandson Sir Robert Fitzwalter subsequently obtained a charter of confirmation reaffirming the right to hold a fair every year 'on the eve, day and morrow after the feast of Saint Simon and Saint Jude, and three days following'. This would have been October 27th to November 2nd.

For many centuries the fair was held on Fair Green or Cock Street Green as it was originally known. As the name might imply, along with all the usual crafts and produce on sale, there was also a livestock market and all the fun of the fair. In those times attractions also included what today would be regarded as the stomach-churningly barbaric activities of cockfighting and bull-baiting (in earlier times, bears would also be baited), as well as swing-boats, merry-go-rounds and side-show entertainments.

One account, written in 1817 (cockfighting and bull-baiting were not banned in England until 1835 – cockfighting remained legal in Scotland until 1895) tells of 'gamesters, sportsmen and spectators' from all across East Anglia arriving by stage-coach at the Scole Inn where, over jugs of ale, the landlord would lead them in a toast to success at the fair:

> Here in the jovial days of yore
> The mad bull welter'd in his gore,
> The gamesters trembled at his roar,
> In the old days of Diss Fair.
>
> A cock, a bull, a surly bear,
> A cur toss'd yelping in the air –
> These were the frolics of the fair,
> In the old days of Diss Fair.

Of course sometimes the bulls escaped. The 1817 report also recounts: 'The bull grew more infuriated than ever, and making one mad, desperate plunge he broke the tether and dashed wildly among the people. I shall never forget the scene. The bravest men turned pale, and the terror of the women and children was dreadful to behold.

> The mob scampered in all directions like an army put to
> flight, and the Green was in a moment the scene of utter
> confusion – apple-stalls lay over-turned upon their
> owners; the *tymbesters* (dancers and musicians) and
> mountebanks threw down their instruments and fled for
> their lives; and to crown all a fearful thunderstorm, which
> had been threatening since noon, burst over the scene.

Following the ban on bloodsports, the fair turned into a more conventional country livestock and agricultural fair. The event also served as a hiring fair for one day – called Chalk-Back Day – when a servant or agricultural worker was marked on the back with chalk when they were hired.

Sadly the priggishness of the Victorian era gradually eroded the more anarchic ways of the Georgian era. In 1863, Cock Street became Denmark Street, to commemorate the marriage of Bertie, the Prince of Wales and future King Edward VII, to Princess Alexandra of Denmark, while Cock Street Green became Fair Green. (Although given Edward's subsequent unfaithfulness to his wife and his notorious reputation as a playboy and philanderer, perhaps the town council should have stuck with the original name.) Then, following representations to the Home Office by the Diss Justices of the Peace, who were concerned about rowdiness, public order and the anti-social behaviour of 'a few drunken freaks' (still to be seen to this day on market days in Diss) in 1872 the Diss Cock Street Fair and its frolics was abolished and with that nearly seven hundred years of history came to an abrupt close.

But, there is still a Cock Inn on Fair Green and every spring a travelling fun fair visits the Green for three days.

QUITE
INTRIGUING
TOO

Rowdy Sports in Diss

You can have some sympathy for the Victorian authorities' concerns about maintaining public order at Diss Fair as *Dissians* do seemed to have been a rather rowdy lot.

For example, there is an account of a game of 'camping' or camp-ball (a form of no-rules football played from medieval times through to the nineteenth century) that took place on Diss Common in the 1740s between teams from Norfolk and Suffolk. There were three hundred men on each side, the game went on for fourteen hours and nine people were killed or subsequently died from their injuries.

As a contemporary observer commented 'The contest for the ball never ends without black eyes and bloody noses, broken heads or shins, and some serious mischief.' In later years the rules (what few rules there were that is) were amended to ban fisticuffs during the game.

And the Elephant?

By way of a curious footnote to the story of Fair Green, in early November 2019 (just as I was beginning to write this book) BBC Norfolk reported geophysics students from the University of East Anglia had conducted a survey using ground-penetrating radar and found evidence supporting a local legend of a circus elephant having been buried there in 1946. There are also reports that a century earlier an elephant, visiting with a touring menagerie, had been cremated on the green after it died. At the time of publication, the UEA team are still considering whether to conduct a full archaeological dig to investigate the elephant's graveyard as well as other historical features.

The Two Sides of the Town Sign

For a small South Norfolk market town, Diss has a surprising poetry legacy, stretching back to the reign of Henry VIII and the poet John Skelton (1460–1529). Born in or near Diss he was related to Sir John Shelton whose wife was Anne Boleyn's aunt.

John the poet's own involvement with the Tudor court began in the latter years of the fifteenth century, when he was a tutor (or *scolemaster*) to the young Prince Henry (later Henry VIII) and reportedly taught the prince how to spell. In 1498 John was ordained a priest and in about 1504, he became the Rector of Diss, in charge of the parish church of St Mary's, a post he held until his death, although from 1512 onwards he lived in London.

According to some accounts, John Skelton had already served as the poet to King Henry VII (Prince Henry's father) and when Henry succeeded to the throne as Henry VIII, he was also granted the title of *Orator Regius*. Later still, Skelton would sign himself as Poet Laureate although the exact status and validity of this latter title has been disputed.

What sort of poetry did John Skelton write to earn these honours? Although the philosopher Erasmus described him as 'the incomparable light and glory of English letters', Skelton was better-known at the time for his satirical and comic verse. On occasions his verse was so scurrilous that it made him enemies both within the church and at court. In fact Skelton spent the last seven years of his life living (and hiding) within the precincts of Westminster Abbey, taking advantage of the sanctuary it offered to avoid being arrested by Cardinal Wolsey.

After his death, Skelton's reputation rapidly crumbled and within less than a century he was being described as a 'rude rayling rimer' who merely wrote doggerel, while Alexander Pope would later call him that 'beastly Skelton'. The man himself was modest about his own work:

> For though my ryme be ragged,
> Tattered and jagged,
> Rudely rayne beaten,
> Rusty and moughte [moth] eaten,
> It hath in it some pith.

In one of those quirks of fate, by the twentieth century, while many of Skelton's contemporaries and critics had been forgotten, his own reputation had been reassessed and his verse structure – known as *Skeltonics*, which employs short lines with rapid, tumbling rhymes – was being compared to modern rap, as can be seen from these lines from Skelton's poem *Ware the Hawk*...

> He shall be as now nameless,
> But he shall not be blameless,
> Nor he shall not be shameless;
> For sure he wrought amiss
> To hawk in my church of Diss.

What about the poor parishioners of Diss, who Skelton abandoned for the last seventeen years of his life? As it happens, it would seem his congregation were glad to see the back of him, as they were scandalised by his activities, which included turning up for church services accompanied by his wife (technically his mistress – priests at this time were supposed to be celibate) and two children.

Eventually the parishioners complained and Skelton was summoned to the Bishop's Palace to explain his actions to Bishop Richard Nix. The meeting did not go well, despite the fact Skelton brought along two chickens to give to the bishop as a gift – or perhaps as a bribe. It culminated with Skelton saying to the bishop...

> My Lord, my capons have proper names. This capon is
> Alpha – this is the first capon that I did ever give you.
> And this other capon is called Omega – and this is the
> last capon that ever I will give to you and so fare you
> well!

Nix temporarily suspended Skelton as Rector of Diss and Skelton never went back to the parish (although he continued to draw the income from his benefice for the rest of his life), returning shortly afterwards to London and the court of Henry VIII.

Skelton is buried is St Margaret's Church, next to Westminster Abbey in London, but the town sign in Diss, by the mouth of the Mere, continues to celebrate his connection with the town, with one side depicting Skelton teaching the young Prince Henry. Incidentally, John Skelton is credited with having first coined the phrases 'By hook or by crook' and 'I smell a rat'.

There is also a second Poet Laureate associated with Diss, namely John Betjeman (1906–1984). Betjeman first came to Diss in 1963 when he was making a TV series for the BBC on English market towns. The programme, *Something About Diss*, aired in 1964 and Betjeman, who described Diss as his favourite Norfolk town, subsequently struck up a friendship with Mary Wilson, the wife of the then British Prime Minister Harold Wilson. Mrs Wilson (later the Baroness Wilson of Rievaulx, who died in June 2018 at the age of 102) was born in Diss in 1916 and grew up in the local area. Betjeman's fondness of Diss and friendship with Mary Wilson inspired his own well-known poem *A Mind's Journey to* Diss (written *circa* 1966) describing an imaginary train journey from London to Diss. The poem opens with the following lines:

Dear Mary,
Yes, it will be bliss
To go with you by train to Diss,

And ends with:

The train slows down into a crawl
And stops in silence... Where is this?
Dear Mary Wilson, this is Diss.

QUITE
INTRIGUING
TOO

An Infamous Daughter of Diss

If Mary Wilson was one of Diss's most famous daughters, then to maintain the balance, mention must be made of the town's most infamous daughter. Born in Diss in 1883, Ethel Le Neve is best known to history as the mistress of the poisoner Dr Harvey Crippen. Crippen's wife Cora, a.k.a. Belle Elmore, went missing in January 1910 and, following a transatlantic boat chase, Crippen was arrested in Canada, brought back to England, put on trial for her murder, convicted and executed in November of that year.

Disguised, somewhat implausibly, as a boy, Ethel Le Neve accompanied Crippen on the ill-fated attempt to flee to North America and subsequently stood trial at the Old Bailey on a charge of being an accessory after the fact. She was acquitted and immediately emigrated to Canada, leaving England by boat the same morning Crippen was executed. She later returned to London under a new name, married, had two children, and died in Croydon in 1967. As a popular song of the time had it,

Doctor Crippen killed Belle Elmore
Ran away with Miss Le Neve
Right across the Ocean Blue
Followed by Inspector Dew*
Ship's ahoy, Naughty Boy!

* The arresting police officer was Chief Inspector Walter Dew of Scotland Yard.

Still on the subject of women and murder, Louie's Lane at the Roydon end of Diss takes its name from Louie Bryant, who may or may not have been a woman of easy virtue, who was brutally murdered (and therefore unable to defend her reputation) in September 1829 after attending a barn dance. There is a suggestion she left the barn to meet with a stranger who had approached her at the dance but Louie never lived to tell her side of the story, as the following morning she was found lying dead in the lonely lane that now bears her name.

She had been repeatedly stabbed. The murder weapon, a knife, was found in an adjoining field and the parish authorities interviewed over forty people during the course of a six-day investigation. Even Louie's estranged husband, then living in London, was brought back to Diss and forced to undergo the ordeal of touching her corpse with his hands. There was a belief in those days, technically called cruenation, that if a murderer touched the body of their victim, the corpse would spontaneously start to bleed, as it was God's way of revealing the guilty.

To the disappointment of the investigators, nothing happened and the husband was allowed to go free and, to this day, her murder remains unsolved. The last we hear of poor Louie Bryant was that her blood-stained, knife-gashed clothing was put on display in a local shop and remained on there on show for the next forty years until it was finally burned.

The Other Side of the Town Sign:

Bad King John and the Chaste Lady Matilda

Still on the subject of murders most foul, let us return to the Diss town sign. On one side is a scene depicting John Skelton teaching the young Prince Henry but the obverse shows a lady in a long pink gown, wearing a tall conical headdress (technically a 'hennin'). Standing next to her is a distinguished-looking, bearded gentleman in black medieval garb, offering the woman what appears to be a boiled egg, in an eggcup.

The Diss town sign, with poisoned egg. Photo: Charles Christian.

The plaque on the sign's base explains the image shows Matilda, the daughter of Sir Robert Fitzwalter (that's the son of Sir Walter Fitz-Robert who first established the fair), who rejected the advances of King John and, as a consequence, the angry King sent a messenger bearing the gift of 'a poisoned potched egg, whereof she died in 1213'. A 'potched' egg is another name for a boiled egg, rather than a poached one. (Given early thirteenth century culinary hygiene, potched eggs were notorious for causing food poisoning.)

This is an intriguing tale as it reveals how, over the centuries, two entirely separate stories, aided and abetted by some sixteenth and seventeenth century playwrights, have become intermingled to create an urban myth.

The facts are Sir Robert Fitzwalter did have a daughter called Matilda and, in a statement he made in 1212, he claimed King John had attempted to seduce her. King John was a notorious womaniser and several other barons made similar allegations against him. We know Sir Robert, also called Robert the Valiant, was one of the barons challenging King John's powers: he was one of the signatories of the Magna Carta and he fought against John in the subsequent civil war of 1215–17.

Sir Robert later made peace with the crown, went on a crusade, and eventually died in his bed in 1235, by which time he was regarded as a champion of English liberty and 'renowned for his martial deeds'.

Over time Sir Robert and his daughter Matilda became caught up in the legend of Robin Hood so that, by the early 1600s, one play – the snappily titled *The Downfall of Robert, Earl of Huntingdon, afterwards called Robin Hood, with his Love to Chaste Matilda, the Lord Fitzwalter's daughter, afterwards his faire Maid Marian* – depicted Matilda fleeing from King John's lustful advances, escaping to Sherwood Forest, changing her name, and eventually becoming Robin Hood's companion Maid Marian. Another play – *King John and Matilda* in 1628 – sees her constantly falling into the hands of King John, only to escape with her virtue intact.

In both plays she is ultimately murdered, a martyr to virtue, by the agents of King John. In one she falls prey to a poisoned glove, while in the other it is a bracelet whose poison had 'eaten its way to her bone, and the fiery poison had dried her life blood'.

Talking of poison, King John, according to legend, died as a result of drinking poisoned ale, eating poisoned plums or a 'surfeit' of peaches. (This is in contrast to his ancestor King Henry I who died from eating a surfeit of lampreys.) In reality, dysentery is the more likely culprit.

But where does this leave us with the tale of Matilda Fitzwalter of Diss?

The clue can be found in the 1628 play, where there is a minor character called Lady Bruce, the wife of one of the barons opposing King John. She and her young son George are both shown being imprisoned by John's men and left to starve to death in a dungeon. And this is where historical fiction does overlap with historical fact for in real life there was another Matilda in King John's circle. She was Matilda (or Maud, the names were used interchangeably, also known as the Lady of Hay, after Hay-on-Wye) who was married to William de Braose, a powerful baron on the Welsh Borders who was, for about ten years, a favourite of King John.

Unfortunately in 1208, William quarreled with John. One suggestion is it was over a huge sum of money (5000 marks or £3,000,000/ US$4,000,000 in modern values) William owed the king. Another suggestion is Matilda de Braose made indiscreet comments regarding the murder of King John's nephew Arthur, the Duke of Brittany.

Whatever the reason, John demanded Matilda's son William be sent to him as a hostage for her husband's loyalty. Matilda refused, stating that she would not deliver her children to a king who had murdered his own nephew. John acted quickly and ruthlessly, leading troops to seize de Braose's castles and, in 1210, captured both Matilda and her son William. Matilda's husband, meanwhile, had been declared an outlaw. He escaped to France, disguised as a beggar, but died the following year.

As for Matilda and her son, they were first imprisoned at Windsor Castle but subsequently transferred to Corfe Castle in Dorset, where they were placed inside the dungeon and allowed to starve to death. According to one report, the boy died first and his body was found to be covered in bite marks and the flesh chewed where his starving mother had, in desperation, been forced to eat her own child. Rats are a more likely culprit.

King John then was definitely, as the old history books would put it, not just a bad king but a very bad king. As for Matilda Fitzwalter of Diss, she may have been propositioned by King John but at least she was not poisoned by him. There again, disappointingly for the romantics among us, neither did she run away to the Green Wood to become Robin Hood's girlfriend. Now it is time to head out of town and start exploring the Waveney valley as it heads towards the sea.

CHAPTER 4

MISTLETOE BRIDES AND GHOSTLY AIRMEN: ALONG THE NORTH BANK TO BROCKDISH

Three miles to the east of Diss lies the village of Scole, once an important crossroads on the route from Ipswich to Norwich, where it is intersected by the Bury St Edmunds to Great Yarmouth road. As long ago as the time of the Romans, the strategic significance of Scole was recognised as it was the site of *Villa Faustini*, a fort and/or settlement on the Pye Road (now the A140) between *Camulodunum* (Colchester) and *Venta Icenorum* near Norwich.

Scole was bypassed in 1995 and turned into a quiet backwater but it still retains the impressive, three-storey, Dutch-gabled Scole Inn (originally the White Hart Inn), built for John Peck in 1655. Peck realised its location (approximately twnety miles from Norwich, Ipswich, Yarmouth, Bury and Thetford) made it an ideal staging post in the days of horse and coach travel and, at its peak, forty horse-drawn coaches were calling at the inn every day.

Famous guests who used the Scole Inn included King Charles II, who stopped by for breakfast in 1671, and Admiral Nelson, who stayed there on a number of occasions. Nelson was born in Norfolk, which still refers to itself as Nelson's County. It is not clear from the records whether Nelson was accompanied by his wife or his mistress Emma Hamilton (ditto King Charles and any one of his mistresses) but it is safe to assume neither men shared the inn's famous (or infamous) but long since vanished Round Bed that could accommodate up to thirty (presumably very sociable) travellers at

The Scole Inn, guests are no longer permitted to stable their horses in the bedrooms. Photo: Charles Christian.

the same time. Another of the inn's famous but now-lost features was a giant wooden sign that for the better part of 150 years spanned the entire road.

Naturally the Scole Inn has its folklore and its most famous involves a highwayman – and a ghost. This dates back to the 1780s when a highwayman called John Belcher used the inn as his headquarters and, according to legend, when escaping the scene of his latest robbery, he would gallop into the inn through its front door, then ride up its Jacobean staircase and along the top-floor corridors before hiding himself and his horse in one of the bedrooms.

You can still see a gate on the staircase that was supposedly erected to stop him riding up the staircase and it is said that if you lift the carpet, you can also see the hoof-prints the horse's iron shoes left on the oak stairs. History does not record what the chambermaids thought of cleaning up the bedroom after Belcher had stabled his horse there.

It is said that on certain nights of the year you can hear the ghostly sound of hooves clattering up the staircase and along the corridors. Spooky but the inn also has a far more famous ghost, namely Emma, the White Lady.

In life, her jealous husband accused her of having an affair with John Belcher. Despite her denials (although it would seem Belcher did make amorous advances) her husband refused to believe she was innocent of any infidelity and murdered her. Her ghost still walks the inn and her white shade has been seen in one of the bedrooms, on the staircase and in one of the bars. In case you are thinking of staying there and want to avoid the haunted room – it is easy to spot: it's called Emma's Room.

THE S-FILES

Fast forward just over two hundred years from the 1780s to the 1990s and we encounter more supernatural experiences in Scole when, over a period of three years, it became the focal point for a research project called The Scole Experiment. (Also known, inevitably, as The S-Files as *The X-Files* paranormal series was then airing on television.)

Conducted principally by three members of the UK's Society for Psychical Research, the project involved over twenty sittings with a team of local mediums holding séances in the cellar of a house in Scole. In the subsequent report – *The Scole Experiment: Scientific Evidence of Life After Death* – the authors claimed to have received 'both messages and materialised or physical objects from a number of collaborative spirit communicators.'

The report goes on to add: '... the investigators were unable to detect any direct indication of fraud or deception, and encountered evidence favouring the hypothesis of intelligent forces, whether originating in the human psyche or from discarnate sources, able to influence material objects and to convey associated meaningful messages, both visual and aural.'

Search the internet and you will find a mass of websites and blog posts (there is even a Facebook group) either supporting the findings of the Scole Experiment or else seeking to debunk the project as a hoax or scam. We'll leave you to draw your own conclusions save only to comment that the biggest criticisms of the experiment focus on the methodology of the researchers and the lack of controls they imposed on the mediums – plus of course the fact Emma, the local neighbourhood ghost, never bothered to get in touch.

THORPE ABBOTTS AND THE BLOODY HUNDREDTH

Two miles further along the A143, heading east from Scole, you will start spotting signs for Thorpe Abbotts. What interests us here is not the village but the site of the old World War Two US air force base at RAF Thorpe Abbotts, which was home to 100th Bombardment (Heavy) Group (part of the US Eighth Air Force) which flew B-17 Flying Fortress planes on bombing raids across Nazi Germany and Occupied Europe from 1943.

The attraction of East Anglia was that it was a relatively flat, thinly-populated agricultural area on the bit of England that bulges out into the North Sea, making it the perfect location on which to build airfields that were the shortest distance flying-wise from Continental Europe. It was also a safe place to store large quantities of bombs and munitions away from large towns and cities. So popular was the location that by the end of the war there were 37 major airfields (plus at least another 40 subsidiary emergency and decoy fields) and over 200,000 US Eighth Air Force personnel stationed in East Anglia, earning it the name of The Fields of Little America.

As for the Thorpe Abbotts base (known to the Americans as USAAF Station 139), by the summer of 1943 the American squadron located there had already earned a reputation for being unlucky, along with the unfortunate nickname of The Bloody Hundredth for the higher-than-average number of casualties it sustained. On some raids over a dozen planes were lost (each B-17 Flying Fortress had a crew of ten) and on one infamous raid over Münster in October 1943 just one plane – *Rosie's Riveters* – returned safely to Thorpe Abbotts.

In all, during the war, the Bloody Hundredth lost 177 planes in the course of flying 306 missions. There are three suggested explanations for this. Firstly, poor leadership and discipline in the early days

Eddie the Ghost can still be seen looking out of the first floor windows. Photo: Charles Christian.

resulting in planes not flying in a sufficiently tight defensive formation, so enemy fighters could penetrate the killing zone and pick off planes. Secondly, the notorious 'Wheels Down Incident' when one B-17 bomber lowered its wheels in surrender then apparently changed its mind and shot down the escorting German fighters, making the 100th a marked outfit for Luftwaffe pilots. And, thirdly, just plain bad luck of the draw.

Whatever the reason, other American bomber groups liked flying with the 100th 'because the Nazis go after them instead of us'.

By way of context, the US Eighth Air Force suffered 26,000 casualties in World War Two and a further 29,500 flight crew were shot down and became prisoners of war. One member of the Bloody Hundredth – Robert Kiern – was a PoW in Germany for nineteen months in World War Two and a PoW for a further seven years in Hanoi during the Vietnam War. Now that really is unlucky.

With the end of the war, Thorpe Abbotts was returned to the RAF and, after several years of inactivity, the base was closed in 1956 and turned over to agricultural use. In the years that followed most of the buildings, hardstanding, runways and perimeter tracks were broken up. But in 1977 the control tower and several other buildings, including a couple of Nissen huts (or Quonsets as the Americans call them) were leased to a group of volunteers who set about restoring the buildings and creating what is now the 100th Bomb Group Memorial Museum.

Did I mention the control tower is haunted? From time to time, visitors to the museum report an overpowering presence within the control tower, occasionally accompanied by the brief glimpse of an airman dressed in full flying gear. The sound of VHF radio chatter and the noise of aircraft have also been heard.

Interestingly, this is not a new phenomenon as Eddie the Ghost – as the American personnel called him – first began to appear during early 1944 when he was reported to be seen walking through the walls of the airmen's quarters. Stories of the ghost persisted (Eddie was thought to be one of the pilots who died during 'Black Week' in October 1943 when the group was almost wiped out) with some of the men taking their pistols and rifles to bed with them. Fearing an accident, Colonel Thomas Jeffrey – known as Colonel Jeff – the base commander at the time, banned all talk of Eddie on penalty of court martial.

Today, sightings are less frequent although Eddie is occasionally seen when the tower is locked up at night. It is said he appears at a first-floor window looking out as if to say goodnight. On a personal note, when I visited the airfield a couple of years ago to talk to the museum volunteers, they all changed the subject whenever I mentioned Eddie the Ghost. Perhaps they were still following the orders of Colonel Jeff?

Although the Americans – with the exception of Eddie the Ghost – left Thorpe Abbotts in 1946, the Bloody Hundredth are still in East Anglia, now serving as the 100th Air Refueling Wing out of RAF Mildenhall. The 1949 Oscar-winning movie *Twelve O'Clock High*, starring Gregory Peck, is partly based on the missions flown by the 100th.

BROCKDISH AND THE MISTLETOE BRIDE

Moving on eastwards from Thorpe Abbotts, we find the village of Brockdish situated on the north bank of the Waveney. Brockdish is, incidentally, the highest point on the river where canoes and kayaks can be launched into the water.

Today, one of the many old and intriguing buildings is the village is Brockdish Hall, which was built in 1634 in an Elizabethan style. This newer building stands next to the moated site of the now long-demolished Brockdish Old Hall – and it is the legend associated with the original hall that is the focus of our attention, for this is one of the locations for the tale of The Mistletoe Bride.

According to the legend, it was the Christmas season so the Old Hall was decorated with boughs of mistletoe and holly, and a party was being held to celebrate the marriage of the lord of the manor's beautiful daughter. At some point during the evening, the bride grew tired of dancing and suggested the guests play hide-and-seek. Knowing the house so well, the bride headed off to an attic room and hid herself in a large wooden storage chest.

Elsewhere in the house, the game of hide-and-seek drew to a close with everyone discovered... except the bride. A search then began of the house, both inside and outside. It continued with increased desperation throughout the night and into the following day but no trace could be found of the bride. Had she met with an accident – or had she had second thoughts about her marriage and run away?

Days turned into weeks, turned into months and into years but no sign was ever found of the missing bride. Her father died of a broken heart, the groom went mad with grief or, depending upon the version of the story being told, went off to war and was killed in battle in some foreign land. Eventually the Old Hall was sold and it was only then that mystery was solved.

While clearing out the building, the new owners found an old, locked chest in an attic room. They broke it open and within it they found a mouldering skeleton, still clad in the tattered remnants of a bridal gown, with a gold wedding ring upon the third finger of her left hand.

The poor bride had hidden in the chest but then found herself entombed alive when the lock snapped shut!

Along with Brockdish Old Hall, Shapwick in Somerset, Bramshill House in Hampshire, and Marwell Old Hall, also in Hampshire, all claim to be the genuine location of the real Mistletoe Bride.

So, were games of hide-and-seek particularly dangerous in late medieval times? While it is possible these legends are based on actual incidents, the stories are all so similar a more likely explanation is it is a form of what we'd now call an urban myth, based upon misinterpreted, misreported or misunderstood historical events and occurrences. These include the discovery of human bones in unexpected places or cryptic inscriptions on tombs, such as a grave at Shapwick describing a local heiress who died in 1681 as 'Taken away by a sudden and untimely fate at the very time of the marriage celebrations'.

For further so-called proof, some locations even claim the existence of the actual chest in which the bride is said to have died (both Marwell and Bramshill) although both these were apparently, and conveniently, lost during the early part of the twentieth century. That said, it's worth noting large chests were once standard pieces of domestic storage and rambling country houses might contain many old bridal chests (complete with a bride's initials and date of her wedding) that held the new bride's clothing and linen and which accompanied her when she moved into her new home.

Finally, a popular parlour and musical hall song during the Victorian and Edwardian eras, particularly over the Christmas season, was the melodramatic ballad *The Mistletoe Bough*, written by Thomas Haynes Bayly who died 1839. By coincidence, it was only after this song became popular, in the first half of the nineteenth century, that we begin to hear of various old houses and halls claiming they were the location for the events in the song. So, was this art imitating life, or life imitating art?

Before we continue our journey down the Waveney valley, let's play out this chapter with the words of the ballad…

THE MISTLETOE BOUGH

by Thomas Haynes Bayly

The mistletoe hung in the castle hall
The holly branch shone on the old oak wall.
The Baron's retainers were blithe and gay,
Keeping the Christmas holiday.

The Baron beheld with a father's pride
His beautiful child, Lord Lovell's bride.
And she, with her bright eyes seemed to be
The star of that goodly company.

Oh, the mistletoe bough.
Oh, the mistletoe bough.

'I'm weary of dancing, now,' she cried;
'Here, tarry a moment, I'll hide, I'll hide,
And, Lovell, be sure you're the first to trace
The clue to my secret hiding place.'

Away she ran, and her friends began
Each tower to search and each nook to scan.
And young Lovell cried, 'Oh, where do you hide?
I'm lonesome without you, my own fair bride.'

Oh, the mistletoe bough.
Oh, the mistletoe bough.

They sought her that night, they sought her next day,
They sought her in vain when a week passed away.
In the highest, the lowest, the loneliest spot,
Young Lovell sought wildly, but found her not.

The years passed by and their brief at last
Was told as a sorrowful tale long past.
When Lovell appeared, all the children cried,
'See the old man weeps for his fairy bride.'

Oh, the mistletoe bough.
Oh, the mistletoe bough.

Shuckland

At length, an old chest that had long laid hid
Was found in the castle; they raised the lid.
A skeleton form lay mouldering there
In the bridal wreath of that lady fair.

How sad the day when in sportive jest
She hid from her lord in the old oak chest,
It closed with a spring and a dreadful doom,
And the bride lay clasped in a living tomb.

Oh, the mistletoe bough.
Oh, the mistletoe bough.

Chapter 5

Bloody Hands and a Surfeit of Saints: Along the South Bank

If you head east from Diss taking the B1118 road south of the River Waveney, one of the first villages you will see signposted is Brome. Our interest lies with the former Brome Hall, which was demolished in 1963 because, according to the antiquary and scholar Dr Montague Rhodes James (best remembered today as the ghost and supernatural horror story author M.R. James) during the latter years of the nineteenth century, it was the location of an astonishing act of cultural vandalism.

To set the scene, we need to flash back in time nearly fourteen centuries to the year 630 when a bishop from Burgundy (in what is now France) arrived in Suffolk to preach Christianity to the 'East Angles' of that area. Called Felix, he established his bishopric at a place called Dommoc (or Dunmoc) which – according to one theory – was located at what is now Dunwich on the Suffolk coast. There is an alternative theory that Dommoc was located within the now lost Roman fort at Walton, near Felixstowe – we'll be returning to the mystery of Dommoc later in this book.

Felix lived at Dommoc, wherever it was, until his death seventeen years later and, during that time, he successfully established Christianity in the region, which until then had still been fighting for precedence over Saxon pagan beliefs, and established the first formal schools in the area. Following his death, in either 647 or 648, Felix became venerated as saint.

Now we fast forward 600 years to March 1286, when a huge tidal surge hit the city of Dunwich and engulfed several churches and

Dunwich Priory. Photo by David Taylor.

monastic buildings, including Dunwich Priory, which belonged to the Benedictine monastic order. Before disaster struck, the monks were able to rescue the priory's treasures, including St Felix's own book of the Gospels, and remove them for safekeeping at the Benedictine Order's priory in Eye, which lies a couple of miles south of Brome. Covered in red leather, St Felix's book subsequently became known as the *Red Book of Eye* and, in the years that followed, would be treated as a sacred object on which people would swear oaths.

The *Red Book* still existed at the time of the Dissolution of the Monasteries in the first half of the sixteenth century, when Henry VIII's commissioners – who were responsible for liquidating the assets of the monastic orders – catalogued it as 'an old masse boke called the redde boke of Eye garnysshed with a lytell sylver on the one side, the residewe lytell worth, 20 pennies'. The 20 pennies (8.5 pence in decimal currency) referred to the value of the silver on the book.

The *Red Book*, minus its silver, survived the Dissolution and was recorded as being kept by the Corporation of Eye (the town's local

The Thrandeston Witches. Photo: Charles Christian.

government authority) as late as the eighteenth century. But after that it vanishes from the historical record, with M.R. James reporting in the early twentieth century that the entire book 'had been cut up for game labels' (in other words labels attached to pheasants and hares that had been shot for sport) some years previously by the then occupants of Brome Hall. And on that note of philistinism, we leave Brome.

THE THRANDESTON WITCHES

One of M.R. James' best known stories, thanks in part to it being adapted for television as part of the BBC's classic *A Ghost Story at Christmas* series, is *The Stalls of Barchester Cathedral* which features a trio of malevolent carvings at the end of the archdeacon's stall: a cat, the Devil, and Death. Perhaps James was inspired by the fact that just a couple of miles west of Brome lies the village of Thrandeston, where two of the stalls in St Margaret's church are decorated with carvings of what are undoubtedly witches.

One witch carries a cat, and the other an owl. No information is available as to who carved them or why. They are thought to be late-seventeenth century, so would have been influenced by the witch hunt hysteria that gripped East Anglia at that time.

In the mid-1640s there was 'Witchfinder General' Matthew Hopkins who, in a period of just fourteen months, sent more people to the gallows than all the other witch-hunters in England had managed over the previous 160 years. The punishment for witchcraft in England, it should be noted, was to be hanged, not burned at the stake. Then, in 1662, there was the trial at the Bury St Edmunds' Assize Court of Rose Cullender and Amy Denny, two elderly widows from Lowestoft, who were accused of thirteen counts of bewitching local children. They were found guilty and a few days later executed.

Although only involving just two people, the Lowestoft witchcraft trial was significant. It was presided over by Sir Matthew Hale, one of the most senior judges of the time, so his involvement gave credibility and encouragement to subsequent witchcraft trials. One of the witnesses for the prosecution was Sir Thomas Browne, a philosopher, author and polymath, whose view that witches and witchcraft were real phenomena, undoubtedly influenced the jury. And, the court also accepted the concept of 'spectral evidence' – in otherwords witnesses saying they had dreams and visions in which they saw the witches casting spells on them.

This last point might seem an obscure point of law but it created a legal precedent that was exploited by the magistrates in the notorious Salem Witch Trials in the North American colonies some thirty years later. All in all, some significant consequence arising from a case which originally started with two old women arguing about the price of herrings with a Lowestoft fishmonger.

As for the Thrandeston connection, not only was the Lowestoft witchcraft trial a *cause célèbre* at the time the stall carvings were being fashioned but the two alleged witches would have passed very close by here on their way to stand trial in Bury St Edmunds.

Sir Thomas Browne

Sir Thomas Browne's involvement in the Lowestoft witchcraft trial is also reminiscent of the roll played by the fictional Sir Matthew Fell in another M.R. James short story, *The Ash-tree*, which has also been adapted for television. Set in Suffolk in the 1690s, Sir Matthew's testimony contributes to the conviction and execution of a local witch, Mrs Mothersole, whose dying words place a fatal curse on Sir Matthew. No fatal curse befell Sir Thomas Browne, who died of natural causes in 1682. However when his tomb was accidentally reopened by workmen in 1840, his skull was stolen by a sexton, sold to a surgeon, and kept on display in the local Norfolk and Norwich Hospital Museum for the next eighty years. It was reburied with the rest of Sir Thomas's bones until 1922, when it was then recorded in the Burial Register as being aged 317 years old.

HOXNE

Moving on another mile, our next destination is the village of Hoxne (pronounced *Hoxon*). An ancient and pretty little village, located just off the main road so it is easy to explore on foot, Hoxne is on our itinerary for two reasons: its role in the legend of St Edmund, and as the location of the Hoxne Hoard.

Because the saga of St Edmund is a long and complex one embracing everything from rampaging hordes of Viking warriors to ghosts coming back from beyond the grave to seek vengeance, we will be looking at this in detail in the next chapter. But what of the Hoxne Hoard?

The story starts in an unglamorously mundane fashion in November 1992, when a local farmer lost a hammer in a field and asked a friend, an amateur metal-detectorist, to help him look for it. They found the hammer but they also detected and dug up some silver spoons and gold jewellery, along with numerous gold and silver coins. Happily for everyone concerned, they immediately stopped their excavations, notified the relevant authorities and the next day a team of archaeologists arrived to conduct an emergency rescue dig.

What the archaeologists found was that the items uncovered the previous day comprised just a fraction of the treasure beneath the surface. Their excavations revealed a total of over 15,000 items, including 14,865 gold, silver and bronze coins from the Roman era, the largest hoard of Roman coins ever discovered in England. Interestingly, the treasure had been carefully stacked and buried in a long-since decayed wooden chest, with the archaeologists subsequently detecting traces of a wooden post-hole which, they believe, may have been the location of a marker post intended to help someone retrieve the treasure at a later date.

Along with the gold and silver coins, there were also small items of jewellery, cutlery and tableware, including silver pepperpots and ninety-eight spoons and ladles. While the total bullion content amounted to 7.7lbs of gold and 52.4lbs of silver, the Hoxne treasure included no large pieces of silver plate, nor any of the more common types of jewellery, such as the brooches and earrings worn by Roman women, so it probably represented only a part of the wealth of its owners.

When and why was it buried? The majority of the coins can be dated to the period 378–408 and the reigns of the emperors Arcadius (died 408), Constantine III (executed 411) and Honorious (died 423). This coincides with a period of grave political upheaval and uncertainty within the Roman province of Britannia, which saw the Roman legions returning to continental Europe to protect the heartlands of the empire from barbarian attacks (and/or to help their generals pursue their own imperial ambitions) while fresh waves of Pictish raiders swept down from the North, along with the Irish from the

West, and the Angles, Saxon and Jutes who landed along the East Coast, which was already known as the Saxon Shore.

Faced with such a fundamental breakdown of law and order, burying your treasures in a field became the Romano-British equivalent of locking them away in a bank vault or safety deposit box. Hoards of Roman-era treasure have also been found at nearby Eye, as well as at Thetford and Mildenhall, two other towns in East Anglia.

One fascinating aspect of the Hoxne treasures is some items carry the names of the people who either owned them or they had been gifted to. For example the name Aurelius Ursicinus is found on several spoons. There is also a gold bracelet engraved with the Latin inscription *VTERE FELIX DOMINA IVLIANE* or 'Good Luck Lady Juliana'. Living in the times she did, Lady Juliana would have needed all the luck she could get.

There is also one spoon inscribed with *FAVSTINEVIVAS* or 'Faustinus, may you live', which is doubly interesting as the Roman settlement/fort of *Villa Faustini*, which we've already encountered, was just a couple of miles away. The location of *Villa Faustini* might also provide a connection to the Eye Hoard of 600 Roman gold coins, also from the era of the emperors Arcadius and Honorious, found in a field there in 1781.

Based on the dating of the coins in the Hoxne Hoard, one theory is they belonged to a military family (possibly based at *Villa Faustini*) who accompanied the Roman general Theodosius (later *Comes Britanniarum* – Count of the Britains) to Britain in the mid-fourth century, and left when Constantine III and the remainder of the legions abandoned the island to its fate during the years 407 to 410. As the historian Theodor Mommsen wrote in 1885: 'It was not Britain that gave up Rome, but Rome that gave up Britain... '

As for the treasures' original finders, the official coroner's inquest declared the hoard to be treasure trove and the farmer and the metal detectorist subsequently shared the £1.75 million value of the hoard between them. At the time of writing, the Hoxne Hoard is on permanent display in the Roman Britain gallery of the British Museum in London.

SYLEHAM

While the history of Syleham, a couple of miles further east of Hoxne, might not be so dramatic (although there is a watermill that was in use in one form or another from 1020 to the closure of the water-powered clothing factory in 1989) it is the scene of one of English history's many fascinating 'what if' moments.

It was here, in the little church of St Margaret in Syleham, that Hugh Bigod, the Earl of Norfolk (for the full saga of the Bigod dynasty, see Appendix ii) surrendered to Henry II in 1174 at the end of the Great Revolt.

Because Earl Hugh surrendered (and also paid a huge fine to the Crown), he retained his head and the Bigod family retained their estates in East Anglia. When the line became extinct in the early fourteenth century, the Crown awarded these estates to the devoutly Roman Catholic Dukes of Norfolk, who used Framlingham Castle as one of their strongholds. And so it was in the summer of 1553, following the death of her half-brother King Edward VI, Mary Tudor was able to rally an army of 20,000 troops at Framlingham to challenge her cousin, Lady Jane Grey, for the throne on England.

But what if Hugh Bigod had not surrendered? Had the Great Revolt succeeded and Henry II toppled, then the entire history of medieval England (and France) could have changed. Even if Hugh Bigod had died in the fighting or been executed, the dynastic history of East Anglia would have been dramatically altered. Either way, fortune might not have treated Mary Tudor so kindly in the summer of 1553.

In the event, Mary won and her reign halted the more extremist, puritan fundamentalist aspects of the Protestant Reformation that both the late Edward VI and Lady Jane Grey advocated. While Queen Mary I (better known to history as Bloody Mary) was unable to permanently return the country to Roman Catholicism, her successor and half-sister Queen Elizabeth I adopted a more pragmatic policy that laid the foundations for the Anglican tradition that is basically the modern-day Church of England.

From the heritage point of view, the defeat of Lady Jane Grey called a halt to the wholesale destruction of rood screens, wall paintings, clerical vestments, sculptures, altars, stained glass and other decorations that are still such a feature of English churches but which would have undoubtedly perished if the more extreme Puritans had retained power.

Technically Lady Jane was the Queen of England for nine days although she was never crowned. In fact seven months later, in February 1554, she had no head on which to wear a crown after it was permanently separated from the rest of her body by an executioner's axe at the Tower of London. We'll be encountering another short-reigned monarch who also came to a prematurely sticky end later in this book.

SYLEHAM LAMPS

There is a cross memorial near the Syleham church to commemorate Hugh Bigod's meeting King Henry and some nights it may appear to be illuminated by an unnatural night. This light is not the restless ghost of Earl Hugh lamenting the loss of his power but a natural phenomenon caused by the spontaneous combustion of marsh gas (methane and phosphuretted hydrogen).

Also called *ignes fatuus*, because these phosphorescent lights can flicker and appear to move from place to place across marshland, for a long time they were believed to be malevolent spirits or sprites intent on leading innocent travellers to their doom. Over the years and in different parts of the country they go by different names, including Pixie Lights, Lantern Men, Will o' the Wisp, Jack o' Lantern and, around Syleham in the eighteenth century, Syleham Lamps or Syleham Lights. They are of course completely harmless but it is still best not to try to follow them.

Incidentally, in some parts of Norfolk they were called hytersprites, a sort of malicious fairy or bogey used to scare naughty children. Writing in the journal *Folklore* in 1984, Daniel Rabuzzi quotes one woman saying her parents warned her that 'If you go out in the dark on your own, the hytersprites will get you.'

A SURFEIT OF SAINTS

Heading further along the A143, if you take the turning to the south at Homersfield, you find yourself in a part of Suffolk known as The Saints.

These are a group of villages and hamlets, with names that all include the name of a saint and either South Elmham (pronounced *El-em*) or Ilketshall. (Elmham derives from the Anglo-Saxon for a place where elms grow.) Even today, in an era when in-car satellite navigation is in widespread use, you can still get lost. Or, more frustratingly, be able to see your destination across the fields yet be unable to reach it along the winding roads and lanes.

Bad enough though it may be now, spare a thought for travellers during World War Two, when all the signposts were removed to confuse any Nazi spies or invasion forces that might land in the area. In fact the only invaders it confused were all the US airmen based in the area trying to find their way back from social events in Bungay and Harleston. (While I was writing this book, I did encounter a delivery driver in nearby Bungay who referred to The Saints as 'bow and arrow country' – a place outsiders might enter but then get lost and are never seen again.)

So let's meet The Saints... the villages are South Elmham All Saints, South Elmham St Cross (the village has also been known as South Elmham Sancroft, South Elmham St George, Sancroft, Sancroft St George and just plain St Cross– the village church is dedicated to St George), South Elmham St James, South Elmham St Margaret, South Elmham St Michael, South Elmham St Nicholas, South Elmham St Peter, Ilketshall St Andrew, Ilketshall St John, Ilketshall St Lawrence (also called Stone Street), and Ilketshall St Margaret.

Also included in The Saints is Homersfield (the name may be derived from Bishop Hunberht – or Humbert – the last Christian bishop of East Anglia, and an adviser to King Edmund, before the Viking invasion) sometimes also referred to as South Elmham St Mary, and Flixton, which takes its name from our old missionary friend from earlier in this chapter: St Felix. An honorary member of The Saints is

Rumburgh where the parish church of St Michael and St Felix began life as a late-Saxon/pre-Norman Conquest era Benedictine priory.

But why is there such a surfeit of saints? Was this area of the Waveney valley a stronghold of religious activity? At a first glance the answer would appear to be in the affirmative.

For example, along with Rumburgh Priory, there is South Elmham Hall (currently called Bateman's Barn) that was formerly the summer palace of the Bishops of Norwich. There was also nearby Hoxne which, for a few years in the tenth century, was the outpost for attempts by Theodred, the Bishop of London, to revive Christianity in the region. Then there was Flixton Priory, the site of a large Augustinian nunnery.

Well, perhaps Flixton Priory is not such a good example as in 1514, Bishop Nix (the same bishop we encountered in Diss having problems with the poet John Skelton) made a 'visitation' to the priory and discovered the place to be in some disarray. There were complaints the prioress Margaret Punder wasn't providing proper records to account for the priory's finances, and that she made sick nuns get up for the daily matins service. As we learned at the start of this book, throughout the pre-Reformation period matins services were conducted in the very early hours of the morning. There were also complaints that too many lapdogs were present at the priory and, rather more importantly, that Prioress Punder was a little too friendly with her chaplain John Wells.

Bishop Nix ordered that if she didn't provide proper sets of accounts, Margaret Punder would be expelled from the priory. He also said she had to dismiss her chaplain, remove all but one of the dogs within a month, and, ruled that if she ever slept outside the priory dormitory, she had to be accompanied by another nun. This seemed to do the trick. Unfortunately just fourteen years later Henry VIII set in the motion the Dissolution of the Monasteries, which saw the priory dissolved, the building demolished, the estate sold off, and the subsequent construction of Flixton Hall on its site.

Incidentally, elsewhere within The Saints, St Peter's Hall (better known today for the St Peter's Brewery on the site) which does looks like a bishop's palace, is actually a medieval manor house with a quasi-monastic extension constructed with stonework and carvings salvaged from Flixton Priory in the aftermath of the Dissolution of the Monasteries.

THE MYSTERY OF THE OLD MINSTER

Although there is no shortage of evidence of religious activity in the area, it does not explain why there should be so much taking place in what in medieval times would have been a marshy, thinly-populated part of the Waveney valley. To find an answer we need to look at a peculiar set of ruins namely the remains of South Elmham Old Minster.

Because the Viking invasion that swept through England in the mid-ninth century almost wiped out Christianity in East Anglia, there are even fewer monastic records than usual for this part of the country during the so-called Dark Ages. (Modern historians prefer the term Early Middle Ages or Early Medieval Period.) The net result is we do not know who built the minister, why it was built, nor even (because the archaeological record is unclear) when it was built. In *The Buildings of England* guide, Sir Nikolaus Pevsner described it as 'mysterious in purpose and also in date and plan'.

For example, was it built in the seventh century, when Christianity was first becoming established in the region? Certainly its layout follows the design of some of this country's earliest churches. Was it built in the tenth century when Christianity was being re-established after the chaos the Vikings brought? Or, was it built at an even later date, in the late eleventh century, when it served as a chapel for the Bishops of Norwich at their nearby South Elmham Hall palace?

Then there is its purpose, for although it has been referred to in historical records as a Minster since at least as long ago as the fourteenth century, its role in the community has been disputed since the late nineteenth century. Was it the site of East Anglia's second diocese, founded in 673 at the ambiguously named Elmham? The difficulty here is that along with South Elmham, there is also a place called North Elmham, which lies some forty miles away to the north

The mysterious ruins of the Old Minster. Photo: Charles Christian.

and was most certainly the location of the diocese based in the late Saxon period, from 955–1070.

So were the earlier bishops based at South Elmham, in which case the Old Minster is actually the ruins of an early Saxon cathedral? The word 'cathedral' in Saxon times was used to describe a 'mother church' from where missionary priests set out to preach to the local pagan inhabitants. But the mystery of the Old Minster does not end here.

Another question that needs to be considered is why was the minster built in this particular location? There is evidence of pagan Saxon burials in the land surrounding the Old Minster site and there was possibly a palace belonging to the local ruling Saxon dynasty, the Wuffingas, located in the nearby Waveney valley.

Then there is the fact the Old Minster and the surrounding pagan burials were themselves located within a four acre enclosure that once served as a camp for the Roman legions, stationed there after defeating of Queen Boudicca's revolt in AD 60. The Waveney valley, it should be noted, along with present day Norfolk and North Suffolk, was then home to the British Celtic Iceni – Boudicca's own people – one of the two tribes involved in the revolt.

Archaeological excavations suggest the nearby Flixton gravel terraces were a centre of ritual ceremony and reverence for the dead for more than 3,000 years from 2,500 BC in the Bronze Age to the year 600 in the pre-Christian Saxon era. And there is a widely-held belief the Old Minster was actually built over the site of an earlier Roman temple that had been erected in the camp enclosure to serve the legionaries.

We'll be returning to the mystery of the Old Minster later in Part Two of this book but for the moment it is suffice to say this area of the Waveney valley was a focus for rituals and religious ceremonies, both pagan and Christian, for the better part of 4,500 years so it is hardly surprising that we encounter a surfeit of Saints.

THE FATE OF FLIXTON HALL

Following the suppression and dissolution of Flixton Priory during the reign of Henry VIII, the estate was acquired by the Tasburgh family who built Flixton Hall to replace their distinctly more modest accommodation at St Peter's Hall. The Tasburghs were a Roman Catholic family, which prompted Charles II to waspishly comment, after visiting the Hall, that 'these popish dogs have a beautiful kennel'.

Perhaps King Charles had not had a good night's sleep when he stayed at the Scole Inn? No doubt he would have been amused to learn the subsequent owners of Flixton Hall were the Ulster Protestant Adair family

Flixton Hall was gutted by a disastrous fire in 1846 but subsequently rebuilt and extended during the latter part of the nineteenth century to create one of the grandest stately homes in East Anglia. There is even a suggestion the royal family once considered buying it, rather than Sandringham, as a royal residence. Most of the estate's land, which included twenty-one farms, three post offices and two pubs, was sold in 1948, and in 1950, with the house proving increasingly costly to maintain and the estate saddled with death duties, the hall and its remaining land were sold to a speculator.

General Allan Adair, the last of the Adair family to live at Flixton Hall, later commented in his memoirs that the Hall was 'a vast, uncomfortable mausoleum, still with no proper central heating... In winter the children had to wear their overcoats when moving from room to room.'

The end came quickly. The hall's new owner stripped away all the lead roofing, allowing rainwater to enter the building, causing so much damage that in 1952 he was given permission to demolish the building. All that is left now of the former grandeur is the shell of the ground floor, which is used for farm storage, a dovecote, and a lone Giant Sequoia redwood tree.

Before leaving Flixton altogether, mention must be made of one of the properties on what was the old Flixton Hall estate. Called The Dell (it is a private house and not open to visitors) during the late 1960s and 1970s, it was the home of the Canadian poet, journalist, author and all-round bohemian Elizabeth Smart. Today Smart is probably best remembered for her 1945 book *By Grand Central Station I Sat Down and Wept* though during her Flixton years, she was better known locally for drinking heavily at parties then heading home, more than a little wobbly, on her motor scooter. Smart died in 1986 and is buried in St George's churchyard in nearby Saint Cross South Elmham.

Homersfield and Flixton: Bridges and Red Hands

There is a small bridge, now just for pedestrians and cyclists, over the River Waveney at Homersfield. You can find it just down the road from the Black Swan pub and you could be forgiven for thinking: 'So what?' but this bridge occupies an important place in civil engineering history. Why? Because it is the oldest concrete bridge in England.

Now a Grade II listed structure, the bridge was designed by the architect Henry Eyton and constructed in 1870 for Sir Shafto Adair,

The Red Hand of Ulster decorating the oldest concrete bridge in England.Photo: Charles Christian.

Bart, of the Flixton Hall estate. ('Bart' is an abbreviation for baronet or hereditary knight, a now virtually extinct rank within the UK peerage system.) It has a single span of 50 feet (15m), consisting of a wrought iron frame encased in concrete and a cast iron balustrade decorated with Adair monograms. Its pioneering composite construction makes it an early example of a reinforced concrete structure. Road traffic was diverted over a new bridge in 1970 and in 1995 the bridge was restored by the Norfolk Historic Building Trust and the Suffolk Preservation Society.

Before you thank Sir Shafto for making such a magnanimous gesture, he actually had the bridge constructed for personal privacy as part of a larger project to re-route the Bungay to Harleston road so it no longer ran so close to Flixton Hall.

And about those Adair family monograms... For any visitor from Ireland, they must come as a shock as they take the form of the 'Red Hand of Ulster' and in fact in the centre of the bridge you can see the full family crest comprising four red hands (both *dexter:* right-handed, symbolising Ulster and *sinister:* left-handed, as used by baronets) within a shield, topped by a man's severed head. In some versions of the crest, the head is skewered on a spike and still dripping blood.

As to the origins of the red hand, according to one legend (but see the following Quite Intriguing Too) at a time when there was no rightful heir to the ancient the kingdom of Ulster, it was decreed that a boat race should take place and 'whosoever's hand is the first to touch the shore of Ireland, so shall he be made the king'. One contender, seeing he was losing the boat race, unhesitatingly cut off his hand, threw the bloodied appendage, presumably with his remaining good hand, onto the shore and thus claimed the kingship.

QUITE INTRIGUING TOO

Alternative Explanations for the Red Hands

There is an information board by the Homersfield Bridge which reads:

> The legend of the design tells of a young ostler who was beaten so badly by his master that he died from his punishment. Before dying, the boy left a bloody handprint on the wall as a testimony of the assault. In those days the manslaughter of a servant was socially frowned upon and it was held that Adair should not go without some form of reproach. So it was that the sign of the red hand was added to the crest as a penance to commemorate the wicked deed.

It is a wonderful story but sadly an urban myth, with exactly the same story being told about at least three other English families who feature the red hand of Ulster in their coat of arms.

There is, incidentally, another legend associated with Homersfield Bridge which says a ghost was laid (as in 'laid to rest' to stop it haunting the living) under the bridge and that as long as water continues flow beneath the arch, it will remain imprisoned there.

While the Adair family origins are to be found in Scotland, in the early seventeenth century some members moved to Northern Ireland as part of the 'Plantation of Ulster' – in effect an attempt to colonise parts of Roman Catholic Ireland with 'loyal' Protestant settlers from England and Scotland. As one of the incentives, King James I created a new form of hereditary knighthood called a baronetcy. The Adair baronetcy is now extinct, ending with the death of the sixth baronet, General Allan Adair, in 1988.

The Irish connection also explains another unusual event in the hall's history. The year was 1886 and the Flixton Hall estate had a new land agent (today he might be termed an estate manager) by the name of Captain Charles Boycott. Born in Norfolk (and subsequently buried there after his death in 1897) Charles Boycott is best known to history for the Lough Mask *cause célèbre*, when he was the land agent for an English landlord with an extensive estate in County Mayo, Ireland.

Boycott was already disliked by his tenants and farm labourers, with whom he had clashed over a number of issues (including fining them if they left gates open or allowed their chickens to wander) but matters came to a head in September 1880 when he attempted to have eviction orders served on eleven of the tenants.

Their response was to mount a campaign of social ostracism (or 'sending to Coventry') against Boycott, which involved not only nobody speaking to him but also nobody working for him or helping him in any way. All his servants and farm labourers quit and within a week he was compelled to have food and provisions brought in by boat from the other side of a lough because none of the local shopkeepers would serve him.

Boycott's biggest problem was the year's potato crop was still in the ground and at risk of rotting unless it was harvested. Following a letter to *The Times* newspaper, Boycott was able to drum up official government support and a group of labourers from another part of Ireland, protected by a regiment of the 19th Royal Hussars and more than 1,000 policemen with the Royal Irish Constabulary, were able to harvest the crop. It is estimated it cost over £10,000 to harvest about £500 worth of crops (at 1880 prices).

At the end of November, Boycott and his family (travelling in a military ambulance because no driver could be found for the private carriage they had hired) left the Lough Mask estate, escorted for their own safety by a troop of hussars, and on December 1st Boycott returned to England. Boycott's subsequent life in at Flixton was uneventful and he died peacefully in his bed in 1897, by which time the verb 'to boycott' had already become firmly established as part of the English language (and also the Dutch, French, German, Polish and Russian languages).

Chapter 6

The Strange Death and Adventurous Afterlife of King Edmund

Over the past couple of decades there have been several public campaigns in the UK to drum up support for removing St George as the patron saint of England and replacing him with St Edmund, the man who was the country's original heavenly patron for over four hundred years from the early tenth century. Both campaigns failed but they did serve to reignite interest in St Edmund. So who was he and what was his story?

The setting is the Saxon kingdom of the East Angles, which occupied modern-day Norfolk, Suffolk and part of the Lincolnshire Fens, in the year 869. On the throne is King Edmund, a young and devout Christian monarch, who was only fourteen years old at the time he was crowned on Christmas Day 855.

For the previous sixty years, Viking raiders from Scandinavia had been carrying out ever more bloody hit-and-run attacks on England but in 865 thousands of Danish and Norwegian Vikings, described in the *Anglo-Saxon Chronicle* as the Great Heathen Army, landed in their longships along the coast of Suffolk and launched an all-out invasion.

History says the king was on a pilgrimage at this crucial time so in his absence, his courtiers and *ealdormen* (nobles) supplied the Vikings with horses, both as a bribe to deter them from looting and pillaging the local area but also as a none-too subtle hint for them to move out of East Anglia and raid other parts of the country.

Edmund as depicted in the early 14th-century Genealogical Roll of the Kings of England.

Such apparently treacherous disloyalty in the face of a common foe might seem shocking by modern standards but there was no love lost between the England's seven rival Saxon kingdoms. (The Anglo-Saxon heptarchy comprised four main kingdoms: Northumbria, Wessex, Mercia, and East Anglia, along with three smaller kingdoms: Kent, Essex, and Sussex.) This was particularly so in East Anglia where, over the previous two centuries, several of its monarchs had been deposed, executed, murdered or killed in battle by rulers of the other kingdoms.

The East Anglian bribery stratagem certainly seems to have worked and, for the next few years, the Vikings fought their way up and down England, destroying the old dynasties and eventually creating their own separate province, known as the Danelaw, across the north and east of the country.

Among the Saxon rulers overthrown was King Aella of Northumbria who was killed in battle outside the city of York in March 867. (In Saxon times Northumbria meant all the land north of the River Humber and south of the Scottish border.) And at this point we must pause our narrative for a brief comparison of almost contemporaneous historical chronicles written by Saxon churchmen versus the Norse sagas, which were composed by poets some two to three centuries later primarily as entertainment.

As already mentioned, according to the *Anglo-Saxon Chronicle*, King Aella was slain in battle. However according to the Norse sagas, he was hunted down by the sons of the legendary (legendary in the sense there is debate as to whether he actually existed or was merely invented by the saga poets) Viking hero Ragnar Lodbrok (or Lothbrok) who Aella had executed by having him thrown into a pit of venomous snakes. The name Lodbrok incidentally means hairy-breeches, a nickname Ragnar earned when he clad himself in the skin of a bear to protect himself from the poisonous breath of a dragon (I said he was a legend) he subsequently fought and killed.

The Vikings of the Great Heathen Army, who had a long memory for grievances took their revenge on King Aella by subjecting him to the ritual of the Blood Eagle. This was a prolonged torture leading to death, involving disembowelling, evisceration, and pulling the victim's lungs over his shoulders so they looked like the blood-stained folded wings of an eagle.

It's worth noting there is also some controversy as to whether the Blood Eagle was an actual historical ritual or merely a literary device created by the authors of the Norse sagas and later embellished by Victorian-era writers for maximum horror. The revisionists, who tend to take the view Vikings were misunderstood economic migrants on the receiving end of a bad press from contemporary Christian monastic chroniclers, will tell you the concept of the Blood Eagle was just a mistake in translation. There is also a suggestion the phrase refers to the Viking habit of leaving their foes lying dead, face-down on a battlefield, for their backs to be torn open by birds scavenging for carrion. But, as we'll see in this and later stories, the Vikings fully deserve their traditional reputation for being bloodthirsty psychopaths. For now though, let's return to the Great Heathen Army.

After ravaging the rest of England for the better part of five years, the Vikings returned to East Anglia, attacking the kingdom's towns and slaughtering its population. This time the offer of bribes did not work, there was to be no peace treaty, and in November 869 (some chronicles say the year was 870 but that may just be a dating issue) King Edmund's army met the Vikings in battle near the town of Thetford. In the words of the *Anglo-Saxon Chronicle*, the Great Heathen Army 'rode across Mercia into East Anglia, and took winter-quarters at Thetford; and that winter King Edmund fought against them, and the Danish took the victory and conquered all that land'.

THE MORTAL FATE OF KING EDMUND

Among the leaders of the Great Heathen Army were two warriors called Ivar the Boneless (also known as Hyngwar – it is thought Ivar suffered from the genetic bone condition *osteogenesis imperfecta* a.k.a. brittle bone disease) and Ubbe. They were two of the many sons of the Ragnar Lodbrok we met earlier. (In the 1958 movie *The Vikings*, Ragnar was played by Ernest Borgnine and his sons by Tony Curtis and Kirk Douglas. In 2013–2021 *Vikings* TV series, Ragnar was played by Travis Fimmel, Ivar by Alex Høgh Andersen and Ubbe (or Ubba) by Jordan Patrick Smith.)

In the aftermath of the defeat, Edmund and some of his retainers fled east but became separated about twenty miles away, near a settlement called *Haegelisdun*, where Edmund was captured by the Vikings who discovered him hiding beneath a bridge. One legend has it Edmund was captured after a wedding party, making their way across the bridge – now known as the Goldbrook Bridge – that evening, saw the glint of the moonlight reflecting off his golden spurs and betrayed him to the Vikings. As he was dragged away, Edmund

The Goldbrook Bridge in Hoxne, the site of King Edmund's capture. Photo: Charles Christian.

placed a curse on all bridal couples who should ever cross the fateful bridge.

Unfortunately for Edmund, the Vikings who caught him included Ivar and Ubbe. Once in their hands Edmund was roped to an oak tree, then beaten and whipped in an attempt to force him to renounce his Christian faith and accept Ivar as his king. When Edmund refused to submit, saying he was 'ready to die for his people and his God', the Vikings duly obliged by shooting arrows and throwing spears at him 'as if it was a game, until he was entirely covered with their missiles, like the bristles of a hedgehog'.

But still Edmund didn't die and still he continued to pray to God, so the Vikings cut his head off. The Vikings threw Edmund's body into a communal rubbish pit, to deny it a proper Christian burial, and then

Bench end in St Peters, Walpole, Norfolk. Illustration by David Taylor.

played football with his head until they grew bored and tossed it away into a thicket of thorns and brier.

Edmund's death occurred on November 20th (still observed as St Edmund's Day) and a few days later, when the Vikings had moved on, some of Edmund's followers returned to the area. They recovered his body but at first couldn't locate his head. However as they searched, calling out: 'Where are you friend?' they heard the king's voice calling back 'Here, here, here.'

They followed the source of the sound to where they found the king's head, protected from scavengers and carrion by a giant grey wolf that was cradling it between its paws. The wolf immediately yielded up the head, then meekly followed Edmund's men as they took the body back to a nearby village. Once it was certain the king had received a proper burial, the wolf returned to the forest and was never seen again.

There are a number of places across East Anglia that claim to be the location of *Haegelisdun* but the village Hoxne in the Waveney valley area is the one with the longest and firmest association, including the site of Edmund's oak, which stood in a field just outside the village until it fell during a storm in 1848.

Reports at the time describe the oak as being 'ancient with a trunk over twenty feet in circumference' within which were found old iron arrow heads. (Cynics say they were merely rusty nails.) The village even has a Goldbrook Bridge, said to be the site of Edmund's capture and which, until as recently as the mid-twentieth century, wedding parties would take a detour to avoid for fear of invoking the curse.

As for the wolf, in 1890 a vicar found an old stone chest in the crypt of a church near Bury St Edmunds in Suffolk. Inside was a collection of bones later identified as belonging to a large wolf. It is also worth noting King Edmund was the last member of a Saxon royal dynasty called the *Wuffingas*, who had ruled East Anglia since the sixth century. The family name is derived from 'the Kin of the Wolf' – so perhaps Edmund's wolf knew it was guarding the last of the line?

The greatest of the Wuffinga kings was Raedwald (ruled 599–624) who, in the latter part of his reign, was the *bretwalda* or overlord of all the Saxon kingdoms and is widely believed to have been buried in the famous Saxon ship-burial at Sutton Hoo, near Woodbridge.

The Immortal Adventures of Edmund in the Afterlife

But our story does not stop with Edmund's death and his burial within a small and hastily built wooden chapel near Hoxne. Within twenty-five years of his death, miracles were already being ascribed to the late king's intervention and even the Vikings, who now ruled the area, were minting commemorative coins carrying the inscription *St Edmund the King*.

A few years later, as the late king's cult grew, his remains were transferred to the city of *Beadoriceworth*, soon renamed St Edmund's Bury (modern day Bury St Edmunds) and the abbey built to house his shrine became a popular site of pilgrimage.

The reputation of Edmund, the king and now a saintly martyr, had received a further boost after the original grave was opened. Not only was Edmund's body found to be incorrupt (in other words, showed none of the expected decomposition, always a plus point for anyone considering becoming a saint as it is a sure sign of divine intervention) but the wounds on his body had healed and his head was once more attached to his body – all that remained to show where it had been severed was a thin red crease on the neck.

The last reported opening of Edmund's tomb was in 1198, when the body was found to still be incorrupt. One account says a skeptical monk tugged the king's hair to see if the head really was re-attached to the body and was promptly slapped by the saint for his lack of faith.

The next twist in the story comes in 1013 during the chaotic reign of King Aethelraed, forever known to English history as Ethelred the Unready. The Saxons and Vikings were still at war and, after Ethelred had been forced into exile, Sweyn Forkbeard, the King of Denmark and Norway, was also declared King of England on Christmas Day.

Five weeks later King Sweyn was dead. The official explanation was he died in his bed from injuries sustained following a fall from his horse. However another version of the story says 'divine vengeance put a stop to his blasphemy'.

The background is Sweyn and his Vikings were not only seizing as much *Danegeld* (what we'd nowadays call protection money) from his new English subjects but had also threatened to burn down the city of Bury St Edmunds and its abbey, as well as slaughter all its inhabitants, unless they paid over an additional sum of ransom money.

It was then divine intervention struck when, in the early hours of February 3rd 1014, the ghost of St Edmund, mounted on a white charger, appeared in Sweyn's bedchamber and fatally ran him through with a spear. According to the legend, although he was surrounded by his Vikings, he alone saw St Edmund coming towards him.

Terrified, he began shouting: 'Help, fellow warriors, help! St Edmund is coming to kill me!' But the Vikings could not see the ghost that 'ran him through fiercely with a spear', leaving Sweyn 'tormented with great pain until twilight, he ended his life with a wretched death'.

You may scoff at this story but six years later in 1020, when Sweyn's son Cnut (or Canute) was king of England, the new monarch visited the shrine of St Edmund and bestowed on it sufficient money to replace the old wooden abbey and fund the building in stone of a grand new Benedictine monastery. Perhaps Cnut was fearful of a similar haunting unless he atoned for the sins of his Viking ancestors?

Sweyn, incidentally, was never actually crowned king of England and his reign was the second shortest of any English monarch. Lady Jane Grey, the 'Nine Day Queen', holds the dubious record for the shortest rule.

Our story is however not yet over, for in the year 1217, during one of the many barons' revolts and rebellions that plagued England during the Middle Ages, a group of French knights stole St Edmund's body (or at least part of it) and whisked it away to the Basilica of Saint-Sernin in the French city of Toulouse. The relics and the saint's intercessions are credited with saving the city from the plague in the seventeenth century.

The next development came in 1901, when the Archbishop of Westminster received some of St Edmund's relics from Saint-Sernin that were intended for the high altar of the new Roman Catholic cathedral then under construction at Westminster in London. On their arrival in England, the relics were housed in the Fitzalan Chapel at the Duke of Norfolk's castle at Arundel. However plans were stalled when the antiquarian Dr. Montague Rhodes James (the writer M.R. James again) expressed concern about the relics' validity. At the time of writing, 120 years later, those plans are still stalled and St Edmund's relics remain to this day remain in a box at Arundel.

There is however another version of the story which says the monks at Bury St Edmunds moved the saint's still-incorrupt body to prevent the French from stealing it, so whatever relics they made off with, they did not belong to Edmund.

Edmund's shrine was destroyed in 1539, during Henry VIII's Reformation, and in November of that year the abbey was dissolved and the monks expelled, taking with them the secret of the location of the saint's final resting place. Historians now think the body of St Edmund is still buried in the former monks' graveyard at Bury St Edmunds, which now lies beneath the tennis courts in the town's Abbey Gardens.

Then along came George

Although the cult of St Edmund was established within twenty years of his death, he was very much a Saxon martyr and saint and, as such, did not sit well with the Norman and Plantagenet kings who followed.

For the Normans, Edmund was a constant reminder that they, like their ancestors the Vikings, (Norman = *Nortmann* or Northman/Norseman) were only in power because they had invaded the kingdom and killed its rightful monarch – in the case of the Normans, this being King Harold who died during the Battle of Hastings. The Norman kings could also trace their lineage back to the first Duke of Normandy, a Viking freebooter called Rollo (according to some accounts he was Ragnar Lodbrok's younger brother) who was doing to France what the Great Heathen Army was doing to England at approximately the same period in history.

As for the Plantagenets, they viewed Edmund as a little crude and old-school, unlike the more fashionable St George, who better echoed their notions of knightly chivalry, with all those romantic tales of him rescuing damsels in distress and slaying dragons.

The decline of St Edmund can be traced to the Third Crusade (1189–1192) when King Richard the Lionheart visited the tomb of St George in Lydda on the eve of a battle. The next day he was victorious and subsequently adopted St George as his personal patron and protector of the army. Then, 150 years later in 1348, King Edward III founded a new order of chivalry, called the Knights of the Garter, and named St George as both the patron of the Order and patron saint of England.

And that is why a Roman soldier, born in what is now Syria and who never set foot on the British Isles, is now the patron saint of England (and also of Georgia, Portugal and Malta, as well being one of the official patron saints of at least another dozen countries with multiple patrons) whereas Edmund, who was English and died fighting for his country, is a historical footnote.

The Alternative Fate of Ragnar Lodbrok

Although the popular explanation of Ragnar Lodbrok's death (if we accept he was a real person in the first place) is he was killed by being thrown into King Aella's snake-pit, there is an alternative version of his death, which also goes a long way to explain why Ivar and Ubbe were so vicious in their treatment of King Edmund.

According to this legend, some years earlier Ragnar had been sailing a small boat on a wildfowling trip along the western coast of Denmark, when a storm had suddenly blown up and swept him far, far away from the coast and across the North Sea. Eventually he washed up on the coast of East Anglia, where he was rescued and taken to Reedham, which is where King Edmund's royal court was based at that time.

Physicians nursed Ragnar back to health and in due course King Edmund and his mysterious foreign guest struck up a friendship, as both men loved hunting. Ragnar was soon regularly accompanying Edmund on hunting trips, much to the ire of the king's chief huntsman – a man called Bern – who became increasingly jealous of the royal favour being shown to the Viking.

Tragedy struck as one day, when the king was travelling elsewhere in his kingdom, Bern challenged Ragnar to a secret competition to test their respective hunting skills. Two men left Reedham that morning but only one returned. Naturally the king and his courtiers wondered what had happened to Ragnar but Bern merely shrugged his shoulders and said he hadn't seen him all day.

Ragnar's fate might have remained a mystery were it not for his hound, Garm. The dog had accompanied him across the North Sea but been left behind the morning of the secret hunting trip, and began acting aggressively towards Bern, snarling and snapping whenever he caught sight of him. Eventually Garm escaped and led some of King Edmund's men to a shallow grave in small, lonely wood a few miles from Reedham. In the grave they found the body of Ragnar, with wounds revealing that he had been stabbed to death.

It was murder – and there was also evidence pointing to the culprit, for still gripped in Ragnar's cold, dead fingers was a scrap of fabric he'd torn from the clothing of his assailant in a final death struggle. The fabric was identified as part of the tunic of a royal huntsman and, when Bern's chamber was searched, the king's men found a tunic containing a matching rip in its sleeve.

Bern was pronounced guilty by King Edmund who ordered that his punishment was to be cast adrift on an ebbing tide in the very same boat that had carried Ragnar to England. It was at this point Fate took an ironic turn, for Bern did not perish in the boat but was instead swept back across the North Sea, washing up on the very same Danish shore where Ragnar had gone missing several months previously.

Recognising the boat as having belonged to their father, Ivar and Ubbe were keen to learn from Bern what had happened to Ragnar. Bern's treacherous explanation was that King Edmund had ordered their father be killed and his body abandoned in a wood to deny it a proper burial – and so they planned their revenge.

Chapter 7

Harold's Stone to Hangman's Hill: back along the North Bank

We now head back to the north bank of the River Waveney and, pushing on from Brockdish and its Mistletoe Bride, we head east along the A143 to Harleston and beyond.

Historically Harleston is something of an anomaly, originally a settlement within the more important parish of Redenhall, today Harleston is a busy little market town, whilst Redenhall has shrunk to being just a tiny hamlet on a quiet by-road.

This does explain why Redenhall has a spectacular Perpendicular Gothic church, with some parts dating back to the early fourteenth century, while for most of its history Harleston had to make do with a far more modest chapel-of-ease (demolished in 1873, and located on the site of the town's now landmark clock tower) and, subsequently, an equally modest late Victorian parish church. The Redenhall connection continues to this day as the full formal name for the parish is Redenhall-with-Harleston.

Like Diss, Harleston has plenty of history – one of the many plots against Elizabeth I was to be launched at Harleston Fair on Midsummer Day 1570 – and many attractive old buildings, such as the old Swan Hotel coaching inn. The Swan Hotel can trace its origins back to 1549 when a Robert Cook (some accounts say it was a Robert Green) received a sum of money from the Crown for giving evidence against his cousin Robert Kett, the leader of the short-lived but bloody Kett's Rebellion in Norfolk earlier that year, and used to it to establish an inn. There is even a suggestion this same landlord received a further sum of money for informing on those planning the Harleston Fair plot against Queen Elizabeth in 1570.

The town's other remaining coaching inn – the Magpie, now known as the J.D. Young Hotel – was the scene of a meeting during World War Two between the British Prime Minister, Winston Churchill, and the commander of the Allied Expeditionary Force, General Dwight D. Eisenhower, to discuss the invasion of Europe. It is said that one stayed at the Magpie and the other at Salisbury House on the opposite side of the road, with a tunnel dug beneath the road so they could meet each other in secret. As you will see when we reach Bungay, the people of the Waveney valley do have a penchant for unlikely tunnel myths. You cannot miss Salisbury House: it has two preposterously tall sequoias in its front garden.

Harleston's most colourful legends involve The Stone, which is currently located behind the Post Office, in a lane – called Stone Court – leading from Broad Street to The Thoroughfare. According to one legend, King Harold Godwinson stood on this one metre high granite block in October 1066 either to address his troops or else to mount his horse, prior to riding south for his fateful encounter with William of Normandy at the Battle of Hastings. As a consequence this stone – Harold's Stone – was the origin of the town's name.

At least that's the story. A more likely explanation, traceable to pre-Norman Conquest times (the town is mentioned in the *Domesday Book*), is the name is derived from 'Herolf's ton' (*ton* is Saxon/Old English for estate or homestead), later Herolveston, and finally Harleston.

Alternative versions of the legend hold… that the Romans placed the stone there although there is no explanation why they might have wanted to do that. That in Saxon times a herald would stand on the stone to warn of an imminent attack by the enemy (probably the Vikings) thus making 'herald's stone' the root of the town's name. And, finally, that a Viking chieftain called Herolf would stand on it to make proclamations, including granting several cottages (the now demolished Stone Tenements in Middle Row) to the local guilds.

On the top of The Stone, you can still make out a cup-like depression. Depending upon which legend you care to believe this was caused by... King Harold's booted foot as he mounted his horse. Or, it was used to catch the blood, which would later be drunk during pagan rituals, of sacrificial victims who were beheaded at the stone by the pre-Christian era Saxons. Or, it was used to disinfect money, prior to the annual fair or weekly market, during the Black Death or Great Plague.

The reality is the Harleston Stone is a glacial erratic that has survived through the centuries because it made a handy mounting block for horse riders. A glacial erratic is a boulder that differs from the size and type of rock native to the area in which it rests, thanks to having been swept along, sometimes for hundreds of miles, by glaciers during the Ice Ages. There's another glacial erratic to be found in the park by the Mere in Diss, this was originally located in another part of the town where it too served as a mounting block for many years.

BURIED WITH A STAKE THROUGH THE HEART!

Heading out of Harleston on the Redenhall Road, just past the sewage works and the turning for the curiously name Hallwong Lane, pull into the entrance drive to the Broken Egg farm café. With the statue of the giant chicken on your right (the Waveney valley has a thing about chicken statues) look across the road to the fields to the north of you. You'll see this area marked on maps as Lushbush.

The name is derived from a hawthorn tree that as long ago 1668 was known as Lush's Bush. According to local legend, the bush is supposed to have germinated and sprung from the wooded stake that was hammered through the heart of a murderer and suicide, called Lush, who was buried in this location.

No, the late Mister Lush was not a vampire. Instead his fate stems from the common practice of burying all murderers and suicides (suicides were classed as self-murderers) on unconsecrated ground, ideally at a crossroads on the outskirts of town, and then staked through the heart, ideally with hawthorn, to prevent their unhappy spirits from ever troubling the living.

According to the English author, clergyman, occultist and all-round eccentric Montague Summers (1880–1948) '...when the ghost of a body issues forth from the grave and finds that there are four paths stretching in as many directions he will be puzzled to know which way to take and will stand debating until dawn compels him to return to the earth...'

A more practical explanation is crossroads frequently marked the outer boundaries of settlements and so were a convenient location for the disposal of unwelcome corpses.

It may sound primitive but the practice of what were termed 'profane burials' continued for many years, with the last such burial at Lushbush being recorded in April 1813. According to the report that subsequently appeared in the *Norfolk Chronicle*: a woman called Mary Turrell had apparently poisoned herself after being accused of killing her newly-born daughter, whose body was found in a nearby pond at Harleston. The inquest on Turrell recorded a verdict of *felo de se* (self-murder) and 'on the same evening about seven o'clock she was buried in the high road* with a stake driven through her body in the presence of a vast concourse of people'.

Today, Turrell's infanticide would probably be attributed to postnatal depression. Apparently the unhappy woman also had another and older daughter called Annie, and a fund was raised in Harleston to send the girl to a refuge for the destitute in London. Sadly this didn't work out quite as planned for in 1818 the superintendent of the refuge wrote to a contact in Harleston to report that 'I am sorry to say that Annie Turrell has been prevented by the Laws of her Country from producing the fruits of gratitude therein'.

This was a quaint way of saying the girl had subsequently been found guilty of committing crimes and been sentenced to transportation on one of the convict fleets sailing to the Australian penal colony of Botany Bay.

> * This would have been somewhere near the Redenhall Road/Hallwong Lane road junction although the layout of the area was changed by the construction of the Waveney valley railway line in the mid-nineteenth century.

The last-known instance of a profane burial took place in June 1823, in London, when a 22-year-old law student called Abel Griffiths, who took his own life after murdering his father (witnesses at the inquest said he was suffering from mental illness), was buried at a crossroads, wrapped only in a roll of old carpet, where Victoria Station now stands. This is in contrast to King's Cross Station, also in London, where Queen Boudicca is said to be buried beneath what is now Platform 10.

The burial of Griffiths attracted such a large crowd that even a carriage taking King George IV to an official engagement was delayed by the burial. Newspapers of the time described it as 'an odious and disgusting ceremony' and 'an act of malignant and brutal folly'. Less than a month later, on July 4th, the *Burial of Suicide Act* 1823 made it illegal to bury suicides by roadsides or at crossroads, permitting them instead to be interred in churchyards or municipal cemeteries.

As for Harleston, the original Lush Bush was chopped down a long time ago although it is said the man who felled it subsequently went quite mad. It also apparently released the spirit of Lush, whose ghost is said to still haunt the area.

QUITE
INTRIGUING
TOO

Not so much Lush Bush as Kate Bush

Heathcliff's concerns for the funeral and burial of Hindley, in Emily Brontë's novel *Wuthering Heights,* which is set in the mid-1780s, has to be read in the context of the pre-1823 suicides law. As Heathcliff comments on Hindley's death: 'correctly... that fool's body should be buried at the cross-roads, without ceremony of any kind.'

The hidden treasure of Gawdy Hall - and a kitchen-sink drama

A few yards further on past Lushbush, you cross the roundabout at the end of the Harleston bypass and drive on up into the village of Redenhall to its spectacular church: St Mary's Redenhall or the Church of the Assumption of the Blessed Virgin Mary, to give the building its formal title.

The church was constructed over a period of two hundred years from 1326 to 1518, when work finished on the impressive tower, visible for miles around and from all directions. Arguably its greatest treasure is a late fifteenth century brass double-headed eagle lectern, one of only three of its kind in the whole country.

The fascinating thing about the lectern is that for many years it languished at the bottom of an old moat located near Gawdy Hall Big Wood, about a mile away from the church. The moat is part of a series of ditches, ponds and associated earthworks thought to have been the location of an old abbey. But how did it get there and why?

The Redenhall church – yew trees, lecterns and Pilgrim Fathers. Photo: Charles Christian.

The Gawdy Family in Fiction

I'm grateful to Ed Parnell for reminding me the M.R. James short story *The Mezzotint* features a character called Gawdy, 'the last remains of a very old family' – who returns from the grave to wreak havoc on the living. Although the incident takes place at a country house in Essex, it seems likely M.R. James had the by-then-extinct Waveney valley Gawdy family in mind when he selected the name for his fictional story. There are no reports of members of the Waveney Gawdys returning from the dead.

The Gawdys were a family of wealthy lawyers and politicians who thrived in Norfolk and Suffolk during the sixteenth, seventeenth and early eighteenth centuries. They built Gawdy Hall in the 1540s–50s and Elizabeth I is supposed to have stayed there on one occasion. The original Elizabethan house was given a Gothic makeover in the late-nineteenth century but then demolished in 1939. Although the Gawdy family ceased to have any connection with the hall after 1662, the area is still known as the Gawdy Hall Estate and there is a Gawdy Chapel within St Mary's Redenhall.

All of which brings us back to the lectern and the theory that it was actually sunk into the moat on Gawdy land for safekeeping, either to prevent it being destroyed by protestant iconoclasts during the English Reformation in the sixteenth century or Puritan iconoclasts, such as William Dowsing, during the English Civil War.

William 'Basher' Dowsing, who was born just a few miles away in Laxfield, visited over 250 churches in East Anglia during the years 1643–4 as a Parliamentary Commissioner with the task of ensuring 'all Monuments of Superstition and Idolatry should be removed and abolished', in particular specifying 'fixed altars, altar rails, chancel steps, crucifixes, crosses, images of the Virgin Mary and pictures of saints or superstitious inscriptions'.

The scope of the parliamentary ordinance was subsequently widened to include rood lofts, holy water stoups, images in stone, wood and glass and on plate, and representations of angels. Dowsing appears to have been obsessed with angels, removing dozens of them in his time or else having his soldiers use them for target practice. Ironically Dowsing's own portrait has survived the past 350 years since it was painted and can still be seen at the Wolsey Gallery in Ipswich.

QUITE
INTRIGUING
TOO

Churchyard Yew Trees

One of the things that struck me about St Mary's Redenhall when I visited it was the number of yew trees in the churchyard, which inevitably prompts the question: why do so many English churchyards contain yews?

There is no shortage of theories: everything from them being planted over the graves of plague victims to purify the ground, to providing a handy supply of wood for medieval longbows. The latter explanation is particularly unlikely as yews are far too slow growing and England's demand for bows soon exhausted all local supplies to the extent that by the fifteenth century there was a thriving trade in importing yew staves from Continental Europe.

The true explanation seems to be yews were planted as hedging in churchyards because their foliage is toxic and, more importantly, because local farmers knew they were toxic to livestock, so had a big incentive to prevent their cattle from grazing in churchyards.

And just remember: No yew at Yuletide! There is an old superstition that it is unlucky to cut branches of yew and bring them into your house as part of your Christmas decorations, for if you do, there will be a death in the house within a year. Although given the toxic nature of yew, this is actually a sensible health and safety precaution.

PILGRIMS AND PLAYWRIGHTS

Before leaving Redenhall, mention should be made of the Fuller Family: Dr Samuel Fuller, his brother Edward, and Edward's wife and son (another Samuel, known as Samuel Fuller Junior) who sailed with the Pilgrim Fathers on the *Mayflower* to the Plymouth Colony, in what is now Massachusetts, four hundred years ago in 1620.

The two brothers were both born and raised in Redenhall and baptised at St Mary's although they subsequently moved to Holland to pursue their religious beliefs. (You can still see gravestones belonging to other members of the Fuller family in the churchyard.) For this reason they are described as being among the 'Saints' on the *Mayflower* voyage, as distinct from the 'Strangers', namely other passengers and crew.

Sadly neither Edward nor his wife (whose name history has failed to record – sorry Mrs Fuller) lived through that first winter in America. Dr Samuel did survive (as did his nephew Samuel) and went on to become a respected church deacon and physician within the community. The Fullers are one of twenty-five families of *Mayflower* passengers known to have descendants in North America today.

Back in the late 1950s, the avant garde plays performed at the Royal Court Theatre in London were frequently derided as being 'kitchen-sink dramas' by 'angry young men'. One of the leading playwrights of this of this era was the late Sir Arnold Wesker, who is probably best known for his plays *Chips with Everything* and the 1958 trilogy: *Chicken Soup with Barley, Roots,* and *I'm Talking About Jerusalem.*

And the Redenhall connection? Wesker met his future wife Dusty Bicker while working at the Bell Hotel in Norwich – his experiences at the Bell (now a branch of J.D. Wetherspoon with a bank attached to it) inspired his first play, *The Kitchen.* Wesker would subsequently stay with his wife's family at Beck Farm in Redenhall and this was the inspiration for *Roots,* a play written in the Norfolk dialect. On a personal note, *Roots* was one of the set texts for my A-level English Literature exams. As a schoolboy growing up in 1960s Yorkshire, a play in Norfolk dialect was only marginally less comprehensible than one written in Klingon.

In a stage direction Wesker describes the farm as 'A rather ramshackle house in Norfolk where there is no water laid on, nor electricity, nor gas. Everything rambles and the furniture is cheap and old.' Beck Farm is private property but from time-to-time is open to the public as part of local Heritage Open Days, when there will usually also be readings from *Roots*.

TWO WORLD WARS - TWO PILOTS

I often take the back lane from where I live in Denton (coming next) to Harleston, via the village of Alburgh and skirting the eastern edge of the Gawdy Hall Estate. By an isolated row of houses on Church Lane there now stands a smart, new war memorial although when I first moved to this area, it was just a scruffy wooden cross featuring some almost undecipherable lettering.

I asked around about its origins and was told it was erected to commemorate an incident in World War Two, when 'a Nazi pilot, who'd been shot-down, was captured, then lynched by an angry mob' enraged by the bombing raid he had just made on Harleston. As this seemed a most unusual tale (and one I was surprised I'd never encountered before) I did a little digging and discovered the current urban myth was the result of a conflation of two separate incidents in two separate World Wars.

In fact the Church Lane memorial commemorates a Canadian pilot, 2nd Lieutenant Joseph Phillips, who sustained fatal injuries when his plane crashed in a wheat field, just behind where the cross is now located, at around 5:30 a.m. on July 20th 1917. Lieutenant Phillips was twenty-one years old when he died and his crash came just forty minutes into his second-ever solo training flight with the Royal Flying Corps.

The theory is he became disoriented and/or encountered unfamiliar technical problems with his Maurice Farman Shorthorn biplane which, even by the standards of World War One, was already obsolete by 1917. Another factor that may have contributed to the crash is the Royal Flying Corps, desperately short of pilots in 1917, had reduced the amount of training allotted to new recruits, so Phillips was ill-prepared for the problems he encountered. There is also a suggestion he may have deliberately attempted to ditch the plane in the field to avoid crashing into housing in nearby Harleston but unfortunately misjudged the distance because of the height of the wheat crop.

Lieutenant Phillips is buried in the Earlham Road Cemetery in Norwich and the original wooden cross, now in the Harleston Museum, was replaced by the current memorial on the anniversary of his death in July 2011. Local businesses and charities supplied the materials and paid for the construction of the new memorial.

And the myth of the German pilot? There was a separate incident in 1940, during World War Two, when a lone Luftwaffe Dornier DO 17 light bomber on a raid over East Anglia was intercepted and shot down by RAF Hawker Hurricane fighters. All the crew, except for the pilot, 19-year-old Heinz Ermeck, bailed out and parachuted to safety. As for Ermeck, he was last seen struggling at the controls of the plane as he steered it away from Harleston, only to die when the plane crashed in a field near Starston. He was initially buried there but his remains were later moved to the German War Cemetery at Cannock Chase.

Apart from the pilot, the only other casualties of the raid were two ponies killed by shrapnel when the crew of the Dornier dropped a stick of bombs on some agricultural buildings they had mistakenly identified as military Nissen huts.

FROM ALBURGH TO AUSTRALIA

In Harleston we heard of Annie Turrell being transported to the convict settlement of Botany Bay in Australia. Then in Redenhall we learned of the Fuller family who became some of the Pilgrim Fathers in the early years of the North American colonies. Now, in Alburgh (not to be confused with Aldeburgh, which is miles away on the Suffolk coast) we encounter a strange tale involving one of the founding families of modern Australia.

The story starts in February 1783 when two men and two youths broke into a widow's house in Alburgh and, in the words of the *Norfolk Chronicle*:

… stripped it of everything moveable, took the hangings from the bedsteads and even the meat out of the pickle jars. They also regaled themselves with wine having left several empty bottles behind them.

They were subsequently caught, put on trial at Thetford Assizes, convicted and sentenced to death. This was in the days of the Bloody Code when over two hundred criminal offences, many of them relatively minor property offences, carried the death penalty. The two older men were executed in April but the two youths, because of their age – they were both under eighteen – had their sentences commuted to transportation to work in the American plantations.

But there was a snag. Because of the American War of Independence from the British Empire (by this point the fighting was over but the peace treaty was still being negotiated) they could no longer be transported to the North American colonies. And that is how one of the Alburgh thieves – Henry Kable (in the records of the time you will also see it listed as Cable, Kabel and even Keable) – found himself incarcerated in Norwich Castle Gaol, while the authorities pondered what to do with him and several hundred other convicts. The two older men who were executed, incidentally, were Henry's father and uncle.

At this point a teenage serving-girl from Surlingham, near Norwich, called Susannah Holmes enters the story. She had been convicted and sentenced to death for 'stealing clothing, silver teaspoons and linen, value £2.00, from the home of her employer.' But her sentence had also been commuted to transportation and in 1784 she too found herself in Norwich Castle Gaol.

The conditions in the castle may have been grim (although the prison reform campaigner John Howard actually described Norwich as having a 'humane regime') but the prisoners were allowed to mix, which explains how Henry and Susannah formed a relationship and why in 1786 she gave birth to their son, Henry Junior.

It was about this time the authorities in London decided the solution to prison overcrowding was to ship all their convicts to the newly-discovered continent of Australia and began preparing the First Fleet to transport them. As part of these arrangements, Susannah and her baby were separated from Henry and sent to join the prison hulk *HMS Dunkirk* (a redundant warship converted into a floating prison) moored in Plymouth harbour.

When Susannah arrived there, in the custody of prison warder John Simpson, the officer in charge of the *Dunkirk* said he only had orders to receive Susannah and turned the baby away. Susannah, hardly surprisingly, was distraught and threatened to kill herself at the first opportunity but then fate, in the unlikely shape of Norwich prison warder Simpson, intervened.

Scooping up the baby, he headed to London and personally lobbied the Home Secretary of the day, Lord Sydney (after whom the city in Australia would subsequently be named). Sydney heard out Simpson and then ordered that not only should the baby be reunited with his mother but also that the father Henry Kable, then still languishing in Norwich Gaol, should also join them.

The London newspapers of the day picked up the story – Warder Simpson being described as 'the humane turnkey' – and a public appeal raised money to provide Henry and Susannah with a parcel of clothing and other goods to accompany them to Australia. The family sailed with the First Fleet in May 1787 and arrived in Botany Bay in January 1788. Three weeks later, on February 10th, Henry and Susannah were among the first group of Europeans to marry in Australia.

After this, the Kables enjoyed a remarkable turn in their fortunes. The parcel of clothing, purchased by the public appeal in London, had gone missing – presumably plundered on the long sea voyage – so Henry Kable sued the ship captain responsible for transporting it. More surprisingly he won and was awarded £15 compensation.

Soon afterwards he was appointed an overseer, then became a police constable and subsequently became the new colony of New South Wales' first Chief Constable. He later opened a hotel called the Ramping Horse (believed to be named after Rampant Horse Street in Norwich), then he set up a stage-coach business, before moving into shipbuilding, the sealskin business, farming, landowning, brewing, importing and warehousing, eventually dying in his bed in 1846 at the ripe old age of eighty-two. Susannah meanwhile made her own contribution to the Kable dynasty, giving birth to ten more children.

In 1988, a family reunion saw five hundred of Kable's descendants meet to celebrate Henry and Susannah's two-hundredth wedding anniversary and the Bicentennary of Australia on the site of the first gaol in Sydney – the one Henry had controlled as the first Chief Constable in the colony.

And it all started with him stealing meat from a Norfolk widow's pickle jars.

DENTON IN THE VALE AND MISERY AT THE CORNER

A few miles east of Harleston, on the A143, you will see signs pointing to the village of Denton. If you follow the winding road past a garage, which is quite clearly a converted engine shed from the old Waveney valley railway line, then up Roundhouse Hill and down Church Hill on the other side, you will spot the parish church – St Mary the Virgin – situated at the crest of a small ridge in a valley.

Apart from the nearby former rectory, the former school and one other modern house, there is no village to be seen. The explanation is in the aftermath of the Black Death in the mid-fourteenth century, when an outbreak of bubonic plague swept through England, the remaining population abandoned the original settlement adjacent to the church and the Dentonwash beck that runs through the valley. Research conducted by Professor Carenza Lewis of the University of Lincoln, coincidentally the daughter of a local Denton farmer, suggests plague fatalities may have been as high as sixty-five percent in parts of East Anglia.

The residents of the village therefore moved to higher, dryer and no doubt what was hoped to be less pestilential ground, which is where the village is still to be found to this day. The 'new' village was located around Well Corner, now called Chapel Corner.

Incidentally, the name Denton (or *Dentuna* as it appears in the *Domesday Book*) means "the settlement in the hollow" (or valley or dene) in common with all but one of the other Dentons in England. This is echoed in the words of an eighteenth century rhyme that ran:

> Denton in the dale,
> And Arbro in the dirt,
> And if you go to Homersfield,
> Your purse will get the squirt!

(Squirt in this instance meaning there were so many ale houses in Homersfield that you'd be pouring away your money.)

But, getting back to the church in Denton... It is interesting both from the point of view of its construction and its location. Originally built in the twelfth century, but with subsequent additions and alterations up to and including the mid-nineteenth century, plus a strong likelihood there was an earlier Saxon church on the site, St Mary's is recognised as being one of the 185 round tower churches in England. Out of this total, 126 of these round tower churches are in Norfolk but why include Denton, when from the front the church appears to have a rectangular, red-brick-built Tudor tower?

The explanation is the church was constructed with a round tower but, during the late eighteenth century, part of the original flint-built tower collapsed and it was replaced with the current rectangular tower. Confusingly, the new tower was built in the late-Tudor style of two centuries previously and, just to add a further element of confusion, the Victorians added the west windows in the Decorated style, plus the top stage, including the clock, in flint and stone.

Not being people to make extra work or expense for themselves, when the tower was reconstructed in the eighteenth century, the builders left in place the remaining part of original round tower, where it abutted the nave, and effectively grafted the new tower on to the front of it, so it now has a D-shaped outline.

As to its location, the Denton church lies on the great St Michael and St Mary Alignment ley-line, which could explain why there has been a church on the site for perhaps a thousand years. But could the site have been sacred for even longer?

There is a report by one nineteenth century antiquarian that 'a significant stone' – now vanished – once stood in the parish 'not far from the turning to Homersfield'. In other words, somewhere near or on Church Hill. So did it actually stand in the churchyard, as yet another example of the early Christian church appropriating sacred pagan sites? And where is that stone – probably another glacial erratic – now?

Given the stone's disappearance broadly coincided with the rebuilding of the church tower, did the builders take the opportunity to incorporate the stone within their construction work? Perhaps they were being thrifty with their building materials and saw the stone as a handy block. Or could they have been covering their bets (and their souls) by backing both the Old Religion as well as the New?

MISERY AT THE CASTLE

Denton's other brush with Waveney valley weirdness is to be found at the opposite end of the village, near the site of the old Norman-era motte-and-bailey castle. Listed as Darrow Wood by the National Trust, the castle was only ever a timber fort on a small mound surrounded by an enclosure and ditch, erected and occupied by the Norman D'Albini (also spelled D'Aubigny) family during the period 1088–1254.

Given the D'Albini family's Norfolk estates were centred on their castle at Old Buckenham, it has been suggested that Denton castle was an outpost to protect their tenants from the neighbouring Bigod family. But seeing as William D'Albini (died *circa* 1139) was married to Matilda Bigod, the daughter of Roger Bigod and sister of Hugh Bigod, the 1st Earl of Norfolk, a likelier explanation is the castle was primarily used as a hunting lodge. Old deeds and the remains of earthwork enclosures suggest what is now Darrow Wood and Darrow Green are derivations of *dearhaugh* and the area was the site of a medieval deer park.

All that now remains of the castle is a battered mound, surrounded by an overgrown ditch. Add in the castle's close proximity of a rookery within an adjacent wood and two nearby grimly-named locations: Hangman's Hill and Misery Corner, and the whole place takes on a suitably ominous, spooky atmosphere at dusk.

Hangman's Hill is a small, tree-covered mound to the east of the castle, reputedly the location of a gallows and a site for executions. Sadly, there is no historical nor archaeological evidence to indicate executions ever took place there. The more likely explanation is the mound is spoil from the digging of an adjacent pond, which was then given the more melodramatic name during the Gothic Revival in the early nineteenth century.

As for Misery Corner, this is located where Manor Farm Road meets the Darrow Green Road. One suggestion is it takes its name from being one of the last places anyone being dragged off for execution at Hangman's Hill would see in this life – and they would clearly not be happy about their looming fate. Another theory is it's linked to a young servant girl who committed suicide there, after she either fell pregnant and/or saw her lover being taken off to be hanged. And yet another suggestion is that a horse-drawn carriage plunged into the pond at the corner, causing all the passengers to be drowned.

The immediate flaw in the executions theory is that, as already explained, no executions ever took place at Hangman's Hill. That said, there are plenty of credible reports of people claiming to have seen a woman's ghost haunting the area although there is some confusion as to whether she hanged herself at Ivy Farm, one of the houses at the corner, or else drowned herself in the pond there. Either way, it would appear to be a classic example of a residual haunting.

Sadly, a more plausible explanation is the Misery Corner road junction, on what would have then been the edge of the village, is another place (like Lushbush in nearby Harleston) where a suicide – such as the Ivy Farm servant girl – suffered the miserable fate of a profane burial and being buried with a stake through her heart.

CHAPTER 8

BUNGAY:
BLACK DOGS AND PURPLE REEVES

The local Bungay tourist office uses the phrase 'a fine old town' to describe Bungay but they are being unduly modest, as in fact it is a fine veritably ancient town dating back until at least Roman times. This may come as a surprise as the prevailing architecture in the town centre is Georgian, thanks largely to a disastrous fire – the Great Fire of Bungay on March 1st 1688 – that badly damaged or destroyed about four hundred buildings. (The writer H.G. Wells took a different stance, viewing the name Bungay sufficiently odd he pinched the name for his novel *Tono-Bungay*, which is about a quack cure-all medicine that exploits the gullibility of the general public.)

If you head down one of the little lanes leading towards the River Waveney from the Buttercross in the Market Place, you will find a unprepossessing flight of steps that take you to the Borough Well. (Well you would if it wasn't hidden away behind a locked gate.) The current well-head is a restored Tudor construction but the well was first built in Roman times and was, amazingly, the town's main public water supply for the better part of 1800 years until water was piped to the town from Outney Common in 1923.

The existence of this single source of water also explains why so much of the town succumbed to the flames in 1688. Well, that and the fact the municipal fire engines of the day were crude, hand-pumped machines only capable of squirting some six pints of water at a time over a relatively short distance – which not going to make much of an impact on a big fire.

A replica/part-restoration built in 2016 by the Museum of London, to celebrate the 350th anniversary of the Great Fire of London in 1666, could only manage to squirt water to a distance of between 15 to 20 feet. But even this was better than the earlier alternative of hand-held pumps – called, appropriately enough, squirts – which looked (and worked) like giant metal syringes. Modern-day 'super-soaker' giant water-pistols, which are sold as toys, deliver more punch than those old squirts.

That said, even when the town had the technology, it didn't always make the best use of it. There's one account in Bungay's archives of a fire getting out of control because the fire brigade couldn't catch the horses, grazing on Outney Common, needed to haul the fire engine to the fire.

One of the other 'old' aspects of Bungay is the continued existence of a Town Reeve. Reeves are a relic of the Saxon system of civic administration, the last traces of which were swept away in the nineteenth century, when the English local government system was reformed. Bungay is the exception to this rule and the Town Reeve is the sole survivor of this tradition in an inland English town (there are still portreeves in existence in a couple of coastal towns, as there once was at Beccles which we'll be visiting in Chapter 10).

Until 1910, when they were replaced by an urban district council, the Bungay Reeve and the twenty-four Feoffees (trustees) comprising 'the most honest, discreet and sufficient inhabitants' were responsible for the all administration of the town's public services, including street lighting and paving, as well as providing money and food for poorer members of the community. Today the Reeve and Feoffees still own and administer thirteen almshouses, the Butter Cross and Market, and the farmlands that had been left to the town in the past by wealthy benefactors.

Two other mottos still used in Bungay are 'Hold to the Old Traditions' and 'Dew (Do) Different' both of which apply to the Reeve. Incidentally, if you ever encounter the Reeve and Feoffees, along with the town Mayor and council, making their way along the streets to or from a civic event, the Mayor will be wearing a red robe, while the Reeve will be in purple.

THE DRUID'S STONE

Lurking in the long grass by the main door to St Mary's Church in Bungay is a rough, moss-covered boulder. Although it might be mistaken for being just another badly eroded headstone, this lump of granite is actually the famous Bungay Druid Stone (also known as the Devil's Stone and the Giant's Grave) – the alleged scene of bloody druid rituals two thousand or more years ago.

One theory is it was taken from the ruins of Bungay Castle for use as a gravestone, while another is that it was a ley-line marker or direction stone. Whatever its original purpose, this stone is yet another of the Waveney valley's glacial erratics but it does have an interesting legend associated with it. This tells that in earlier centuries, if a young woman danced around the stone twelve times (or tapped on it twelve times) then placed her head against the stone, she would hear the answer to any questions she'd ask or wishes she'd made. This sounds like a variant of the love divination rituals that once were very popular in England, with the stone answering whether the woman would meet and marry the man of her dreams, or whether her current young man really loved her.

A grimmer version of the legend says if children were to dance around the stone seven times on August 4th, then the Devil would appear. The significance of this date is it was then that Black Shuck, the demon dog of East Anglia (and undoubtedly the most famous legend associated with the Waveney valley) ran amok in Bungay.

BLACK SHUCK, THE DEMON DOG

Bungay's fifteen minutes of fame – almost exactly fifteen minutes if contemporary accounts are to be believed – came on August 4th 1577 when, during the middle of a terrible thunderstorm (or 'in a great tempest of violent rain, lightning, and thunder, the like whereof hath been seldom seen' as a contemporary account put it) parishioners praying in the Priory Church of St Mary, the town's parish church, were interrupted by the sudden appearance of a fierce black dog.

To quote the first published account (spelling adjusted) of the incident:

> Immediately hereupon, there appeared in a most
> horrible similitude and likeness to the congregation then
> and there present, a dog as they might discern it, of a
> black colour; at the sight whereof, together with the
> fearful flashes of fire which then were seen, moved such
> admiration in the minds of the assembly, that they
> thought doomsday was already come.

> This black dog, or the devil in such a likeness (God he
> knoweth all who worketh all) running all along down the
> body of the church with great swiftness, and incredible
> haste, among the people, in a visible form and shape,
> passed between two persons, as they were kneeling
> upon their knees, and occupied in prayer as it seemed,
> wrung the necks of them both at one instant clean
> backward, in so much that even at a moment where
> they kneeled, they strangely died...

> ... the same black dog, still continuing and remaining in
> one and the self same shape, passing by another man of
> the congregation in the church, gave him such a gripe on

the back, that therewith all he was presently drawn together and shrunk up, as it were a piece of leather scorched in a hot fire; or as the mouth of a purse or bag, drawn together with a string. The man, albeit he was in so strange a taking, died not, but as it is thought is yet alive.

In other words this creature rushed into the church, grabbed two parishioners by their necks and shook them so roughly that it killed them both, then grabbed another man, inflicting injuries so severe they left him lying scorched and shrivelled-up on the floor, before it fled off as mysteriously as it first appeared.

What happened next? Well apparently the same creature then made its way, almost instantaneously, to the Church of the Holy Trinity in Blythburgh, some twelve miles from Bungay, where it proceeded to wreak similar havoc. Bursting into the church in a clap of thunder, it killed two men and a boy, burned the hand of another member of the congregation 'of whom divers were blasted' and caused the church steeple to collapse.

The first published account – *A Straunge and Terrible Wunder* – was written by Abraham Fleming that same month in 1577. Fleming, who was studying for the priesthood, was also an editor and translator for London printing houses and, by the time he died, had become the author of over seventy books. In other words he was a pamphleteer – the 16th century equivalent of a modern-day blogger or poster of not-entirely-accurate news stories on social media.

He'd also not been in Bungay at the time of the incident, so had based the story on hearsay from second- and third-hand sources, as news of the incident percolated its way from the original witnesses in Bungay, down through Suffolk and Essex, and on into London. Today this would be described as an urban myth based on 'foaflore' or 'Friend of a Friend Folklore'.

While Fleming's story soon became a bestseller and was repeated in other accounts, it is noticeable that although two other more sober near-contemporary reports – *Holished's Chronicles* and *Stow's Annals* – mention the great storm, they say nothing of a 'devil dog'.

Rather more critically, even Bungay's own churchwarden's books and parish registers say nothing of Black Shuck's presence on August 4th, although they do say there was a violent storm that caused the death of two men in the church tower.

Elsewhere in his account Fleming says the church clock was shattered and 'all the wires, the wheels, and other things... were wrung in sunder, and broken in pieces'. If we add this to the reports of 'the fearful flashes of fire' it becomes possible to build up an explanation of what may have really happened in that day in 1577.

During the course of a violent thunderstorm the church tower was struck by lightning, as all this happened about two hundred years before lightning conductors (or lightning rods) were in widespread use. The lightning strike caused two men to fall to their deaths from the tower, breaking their necks, while a third was struck by a lightning bolt and left badly burned.

While all this was taking place the congregation, who were sheltering in the church from the storm (this would normally have been a safer option than hiding under beds in their little wooden cottages with

*Blythburgh church door.
Photo David Taylor.*

*Illustrations on previous
page and p85 by David
Taylor.*

thatched roofs) would have been surrounded by falling debris, hearing the claps of thunder crashing overhead, listening to the shrieks and cries of the dead and dying, with only flashes of lightning to illuminate the scene. It would have been chaos. No wonder they thought it was Doomsday.

In the aftermath of the event, there were reports that the door of Bungay church 'were marvellously rent and torn, ye marks as it were of (the black dog's) claws or talons'. Sadly this door, and the evidence, was destroyed during the Great Fire of Bungay in 1688. By way of consolation, you can still see what are claimed to be the claw and scorch marks left by Black Shuck on the inside of the door at Blythburgh church. But let's not allow the facts to get in the way of a good story. As the rhyme goes:

> All down the church in midst of fire,
> the hellish monster flew,
> and, passing onward to the choir,
> he many people slew.

Or, as the newspaper reporter remarks towards the end of the John Wayne/James Stewart 1962 Western movie *The Man Who Shot Liberty Valence*: 'When the legend becomes fact, print the legend.'

The name Shuck, incidentally, may possibly be derived from the Old English *scucca*, meaning devil or demon, or alternatively stem from a local dialect word 'shucky' meaning shaggy or hairy.

Debunking Three Legends

No matter how flimsy, confusing and refutable the evidence, the legend of Black Shuck is so deeply engrained within the cultural fabric of Bungay that it will never die. It is iconographic, part of the Waveney valley mythos but there are other Bungay myths and mysteries that are easier to debunk.

For example, why are the paving slabs in Cork Brick Alley made of brick and not cork? This story goes back to the 1890s when Earsham Street House was home to Frederick Smith, a wealthy solicitor and the then Town Reeve.

His wife was seriously ill at one point and her rest was being disturbed by the sound of horses' hooves and carts' steel rimmed wheels clattering over the cobblestones lining the lane running by the

QUITE INTRIGUING TOO

The Fourth of August

August 4th is also the feast day of the semi-legendary Cornish and Breton divine St Sithney (or Sezni in Brittany, died *circa* 529) who was apparently asked by God to become the patron saint of girls seeking husbands. The saint replied that if he were, he'd never get any peace and he'd rather be the patron saint of mad dogs than have to spend eternity dealing with unhappy spinsters and lovelorn teenage girls. 'Fine by me,' said God and so for the past fifteen centuries St Sithney's name has been invoked for help against rabies and mad dogs, as well as for healing rabid or sick dogs.

side of the house and beneath her bedroom window. Smith's solution was to have the alley lined with cork bricks to muffle the noise, thereby guaranteeing her an undisturbed sleep. It worked and Smith's wife duly recovered her health. While the cork bricks have long since vanished, the incident is remembered in the name of the lane.

Then there is the legend that beneath Bungay is a network of mysterious tunnels. According to tradition, Oliver Cromwell built a tunnel between Bungay Castle and Mettingham Castle, which lies a few miles away to the south-east. There is also said to be another tunnel, also built in Cromwell's time, linking Bungay Castle with the parish church of St Mary's. Glossing over the fact the construction of such a tunnel in the middle of the seventeenth century would have been a prodigious feat of engineering, by the time of the Civil War both Bungay Castle and Mettingham Castle were long abandoned, had been in ruins for nearly three hundred years, and were of no strategic value to anyone. So it would also have been a fairly pointless task.

Where did this legend spring from? The source seems to have been the remarkably successful 1796 Gothic romance *Bungay Castle* written by Elizabeth Bonhote. She was the wife of another local solicitor who had bought the castle for her as a present. (Well, that beats chocolates and petrol-station flowers any day.) Elizabeth even had a summer house built between the two gatehouse towers of the castle (clearly nobody had to worry about planning permission and listed building consent in those days) and it was there she wrote her novel.

You'll not be surprised to learn the plot involves a labyrinth of secret dungeons and tunnels buried beneath the castle, including one running to Mettingham Castle, which the heroine uses when she elopes with her lover the day before she was to be forced to take her final vows and be locked away in a nunnery. The novel *Bungay Castle* has subsequently been praised in modern times for its 'proto-feminist sensibility' as the young women in the story keep their fates in their own hands, rather than wait for some dashing hero to come to their rescue.

There is a curious coda to this story, for in 1934 excavations at Bungay did reveal mining galleries (in effect mini tunnels) dug beneath the castle during the 1174 siege with the intention of undermining the walls.

Although Bonhote's labyrinth of tunnels do not exist – and in fact never existed – this has not stopped the growth of another legend that they are haunted. Depending upon which version you care to believe, they are either haunted by Black Shuck, who uses them as its lair, or by the ghost of Hugh Bigod, the first earl, who is still brooding over having to surrender to King Henry. There is even a mash-up version of this story, which sounds like something Mrs Bonhote might have invented, that they are haunted by Earl Hugh in the form of a large black dog.

Finally, we move swiftly on from black dogs to black horses and in particular Black Bess, the legendary mare belonging to the notorious highwayman Dick Turpin. There is a story that one market day in Bungay in the autumn of 1739 Dick Turpin, along with fellow highwayman Tom King, robbed two young women of £14 they had just earned from selling sacks of corn at the old (and now long demolished) Corn Cross.

'Aha,' said Turpin (supposedly), 'let's be having it!'

To which King supposedly replied: 'No! Tis a shame to steal from two such pretty girls.'

But Turpin still took the money and rode away.

It is a nice story suffering from just two important flaws. The first is that by 1739 Tom King had been dead two years, dying of a bullet wound in May 1737 after being shot during an affray at a pub in the East End of London. There is a suggestion he was caught in cross-fire and may have been accidentally shot by Turpin. The other problem is since 1738 Turpin had been in prison at York Castle and on April 7th 1739 was himself hanged for being a horse thief.

Just as the state of many ruined churches and castles is traditionally blamed on Oliver Cromwell (as echoed in the old music hall song *It's* a *Bit of a Ruin that Cromwell Knocked About a Bit*) so any robbery by highwaymen in the late-1730s was blamed on Dick Turpin.

Incidentally, the two young women must have excelled at selling corn, for £14 would be worth well over £1,600 at today's values, which is a good return for a few hours' work one market day.

QUITE INTRIGUING TOO

About Black Bess and that Ride to York

One of the best known stories about Dick Turpin is his ride from London to York to establish an alibi, a tale which culminates in the sad spectacle of his faithful mare Black Bess collapsing and dying within sight of the city walls of York.

Except this didn't happen in real life. This was a romantic concoction of the author Harrison Ainsworth in his novel *Rookwood*, which was written one hundred years after Turpin'?s death. Ainsworth also started the trend for highwaymen to be depicted as witty, courteous, dashing 'knights of the road' whereas in previous centuries they were recognised for what they actually were: thuggish, brutal muggers on horseback.

Where did the Black Bess legend come from? This was based on an apparently real-life event in the seventeenth century involving the highwayman John 'Swift Nick' Nevison, as chronicled by Daniel Defoe in his book *Tour through the Whole Island of Great Britain*.

According to Defoe, in 1676, Nevison robbed a man at Gad's Hill in Kent at 4 o'?clock in the morning, then rode to Gravesend and took a ferry over to the Essex shore. From there he rode across country to Chelmsford, where he stopped for half-an-hour to rest his horse which was, like the fictional Black Bess, a mare. Then he rode on to Cambridge and Huntingdon, where he took another break, before galloping up the Great North Road, arriving in York in the late afternoon.

QUITE
INTRIGUING
CONTINUED

He then changed out of his riding clothes and, dressed in the fashion of the day, made his way to the city's bowling green and struck up a conversation with some of the gentlemen, including the Lord Mayor, who were playing bowls there. He even entered into a wager on the outcome of the bowls match and asked the Mayor what the time was. The mayor obligingly pulled out his watch and replied that it was a quarter-to-eight in the evening.

This provided Nevison with the alibi he needed, for when he was subsequently arrested for the Gad's Hill robbery, he was able to call the Lord Mayor and gentlemen of York as witnesses to swear he had been playing bowls in York on the day of the robbery. The jury promptly acquitted him, taking the view it was clearly impossible for anyone to have been in Kent on the same day they were two hundred miles away in York.

Taking advantage of the old double-jeopardy rule that you cannot be tried twice for the same crime (this rule was abolished in England for serious crimes, including armed robbery, in 2003) after his acquittal Nevison openly boasted of his ride to create his alibi. He became so well-known for this exploit that King Charles II supposedly summoned him to the royal court to tell his story. Nevison claimed said he had ridden so fast even Old Nick (the Devil) couldn't have caught him, whereupon the king dubbed him 'Swift Nick'.

Sadly Nevison's newfound fame did him no good in the long run and in 1684 he ended his days swinging at the end of a rope in York after being found guilty and hanged for murder.

Still on the topic of highwaymen, at Gillingham on the way to Beccles, there are reports that the sound of chains can be heard clinking on some nights. This is said to be the ghost of a highwayman who used to prowl the road between Beccles and Great Yarmouth. When caught, he was hanged and subsequently gibbeted in chains at the scene of his crimes, as a grim warning to others. The practice of gibbeting (suspending the rotting dead bodies of executed felons on public gibbets either in chains or cages) did not stop in England until 1832.

FRIAR BACON AND FRIAR BUNGAY

Before we leave this 'fine old town', one of the more unusual stories associated with Bungay is the tale of *Friar Bacon and Friar Bungay* – or *The Honorable Historie of Frier Bacon and Frier Bongay* to give it its original title.

This was a popular Elizabethan-era stage play first performed in 1589. Described as a comedy although several people die in duels and an incompetent servant is carried off by a demon to become a bartender in Hell, it was penned by a Norwich-born writer called Robert Greene. Greene is now largely reduced to a footnote in Shakespearean studies. Unlike King John, who died from a surfeit of peaches or Henry I, who ingested a fatal surfeit of lampreys, Greene apparently died from a 'surfeit of pickled herring and Rhenish wine'.

The play, with some of the plot lifted from an earlier book, is set in the Waveney valley (Harleston and Fressingfield also feature) and the Friar Bacon of the title is Roger Bacon, the thirteenth century philosopher and Franciscan friar, who also dabbled in alchemy, invented an early form of gunpowder and later earned a reputation for being a sorcerer. Friar Bungay is Bacon's contemporary Thomas of Bungay, another Franciscan friar, scholar and alchemist. Thomas was born in Bungay in *circa* 1214.

The most memorable part of the plot involves Bacon and Bungay creating a talking brazen head, powered by necromantic forces, that will be able to answer any question put it and help them erect a wall of brass around England to protect it from its enemies.

The two friars were warned by the spirits they raised to create the head that they must not miss the first words the head says or it would never speak again. Unfortunately after hours of waiting, the two friars fell asleep and gave their servant Miles the task of continuing the vigil. Shortly afterwards the head came alive and said: 'Time is'. Miles thought this message was too stupid to mention to his masters so he ignored it. The head then said: 'Time was' but again Miles didn't wake his masters. Finally it said: 'Time is past' then fell to the floor and exploded.

Bacon spent most of his later life studying at Oxford, while Bungay was at Cambridge. Both men died peacefully in their beds within a couple of years of each other in the early 1290s. Despite the legends linking the two of them together in the practice of magic, there is no historical record of them having ever met. But now it is time for us to once more press on with our journey.

CHAPTER 9

LOST CHICKENS, SILKEN NOOSES AND THE ROAD TO BECCLES

As we leave Bungay, we head from the Market Place, down Bridge Street, along Ditchingham Dam, past the Maltings – now a residential development – and across a roundabout, still known locally as the Chicken Roundabout, into the village of Ditchingham.

Motorists should note that although you can depart Bungay by this route, you cannot enter it this way as, despite what some satellite navigation systems may say, Bridge Street is a one-way street. You may also notice there are no chickens on the Chicken Roundabout.

Until a few years ago, there used to be large grain maltings by the roundabout and when some chickens escaped from a nearby allotment, they not only survived but positively thrived on grain spilled in and around the maltings. At one point there were estimated to be a flock of nearly three hundred chickens living wild on the roundabout and in neighbouring fields. Not surprisingly, the roundabout earned the nickname of the Chicken Roundabout and was referred to as such on television and radio traffic reports.

Sadly the maltings closed and in 1999 burned down. For many years a local resident, Gordon Knowles, described as 'one of the last of the great eccentrics' by the local council, fed the chickens on a regular basis until a combination of natural predators, increasingly heavy road traffic, theft and possible poisoning by people worried about avian flu dramatically reduced the flock's numbers. The last six remaining birds were removed and given to an animal charity in 2010. A subsequent campaign to have a large statue erected on the roundabout – The Chicken of the East – was rejected on the grounds it would be a road safety hazard although in 2021 Bungay Council confirmed it was still considering some form of memorial to Gordon and his chickens.

A Silken Noose for a Murderous Earl

Ditchingham Hall (not to be confused with Ditchingham House – see next section) is a large country house located a couple of miles to the northwest of Ditchingham on the Norwich road. It is a private house, currently home to the 14th Earl Ferrers and not open to the public. This is not an issue as our interest lies with one of the current owner's more notorious ancestors: Laurence Shirley, the 4th Earl Ferrers.

Born in 1720, this particular Lord Ferrers quit his studies at Oxford at the age of twenty and headed off to Paris for, according to contemporary accounts, 'a life of debauchery'. Pretty much what students do today although now it is called a gap-year. At the age of twenty-five he inherited the earldom from his insane uncle, the 3rd Earl Ferrers, and with it came estates in Leicestershire, Derbyshire and Northamptonshire, as well as Ditchingham.

In 1752 he married sixteen-year-old Lady Mary Meredith. Just six years later she obtained a legal separation from him on the grounds of cruelty. Another contemporary report said she could not accept his drinking and womanising, lived in fear of his drunken rages and violent outbursts, 'and was particularly upset' by his illegitimate children. The earl, it should be mentioned, had continued his relationship with a long-standing mistress throughout his married life.

Some indication of just how bad the marriage was can be gleaned from the fact Mary obtained her separation by an Act of Parliament in 1758. Before the 1857 *Matrimonial Causes Act*, which introduced the start of modern divorce proceedings in England, just about the only way for a couple to legally separate was by an Act of Parliament.

As part of the separation settlement, the 4th Earl was required to pay Mary an income from the rents of some of his properties and the estate was put in the hands of trustees to ensure this was done. One of these trustees was the family steward John Johnson, who had the responsibility of collecting these rents and paying them to Mary. Not surprisingly Lord Ferrers took a dislike to Johnson, who he suspected had helped Mary with her separation proceedings and believed was paying her more money than she was entitled to.

On January 18th 1760 Johnson visited Earl Ferrers, at the earl's request, at his Staunton Harold mansion in Leicestershire. The two men met in private in the Earl's study but, at around three in the afternoon that day, a furious argument could be heard by the mansion's servants, an argument that ended with a pistol shot. Johnson had been shot by the drunken Earl Ferrers.

Johnson died the following day and the Earl was subsequently arrested and transferred to the Tower of London to await trial, for wilful murder, by his peers at Westminster Hall. In those days peers of the realm could only be tried by other peers, not commoners in a normal criminal court. The trial opened on April 16th and lasted for two days, with the prosecution headed by the Attorney General and the Solicitor General, whereas Earl Ferrers conducted his own defence, as all criminal defendants did in those days.

The Ferrers family persuaded the earl to plead insanity, which may have appeared an easy option as almost everyone who knew him thought he was mad. As already mentioned, insanity did run in the family. The family's opinion seems to have been primarily motivated by their concerns for their own reputation, it being thought better to have a murderous madman in the family than a common killer. The earl subsequently admitted he only pleaded insanity to oblige the family and that he was ashamed of this defence as he felt shooting Johnson was justified. Which, ironically, in a *Catch-22* way, does suggest he really was insane.

One of the witnesses called was a groom called Peter Williams, who had once looked after one of the earl's horses but Ferrers was so dissatisfied with Williams' services that the earl seriously injured him with a sword and then hit his wife. In a disturbing insight on the social values of the day, the Solicitor General said this was not proof of insanity or even eccentric behaviour, adding that if a man couldn't take such action against negligent servants, then all the peers present would be in the dock!

At the end of the trial, Earl Ferrers was held to be legally sane (or as one of the peers present commented 'not mad enough') and guilty of murder. The only punishment was a public hanging at Tyburn, which appalled Ferrers as this was the death of a common criminal so he actually petitioned the king to be allowed to be beheaded instead. As beheading was no longer a legally available punishment for murder (only for treason committed by a peer) Ferrers' petition was rejected.

On the day of his execution, May 5th 1760, both the authorities and Earl Ferrers put on a good show for the 'large a mob that had collected because the people had never seen a lord hanged before.' Ferrers was driven from the Tower of London to Tyburn (modern day Marble Arch) in his own coach pulled by six horses. His coach was accompanied by several other carriages, including a mourning coach carrying his friends, along with a hearse and a troop of cavalry.

The authorities had also constructed a special new gallows, with the scaffold platform tastefully covered in black baize cloth and featuring a nice new black cushion for the earl to kneel on when he said his final prayers. The earl wore the same outfit he had worn at his wedding, a light coloured satin suit embroidered with silver and, as a concession to his rank, it is said the rope used was of silk rather than common hemp.

He was hanged by the neck until dead and, later that day his body was taken down, placed in a coffin and transported to Surgeon's Hall, where it was dissected and put on public display for three days before being returned to his family for burial. Lord Ferrers, incidentally, has the dubious distinction of being the last English peer to be executed. Our next story also involves a death by hanging, albeit in even less salubrious circumstances.

THE RIDER HAGGARD CONNECTION

There may be no trace of the 4th Earl Ferrers at Ditchingham today however there are plenty of reminders of another famous local family: the Rider Haggards, who lived, farmed and, in the case of the author Sir Henry Rider Haggard, wrote blockbuster novels while living in the area.

For an author who was writing well over a century ago (he died in 1925) his best known novels *King Solomon's Mines* (featuring his proto-Indiana Jones hero Allan Quatermain) and *She* (featuring his female protagonist Queen Ayesha: 'she who must be obeyed') are still widely read and have been adapted for movies at least sixteen times between them. The earliest version of a cinematic version of *She* was released as long ago as 1899. Rider Haggard's 1899 book on rural life, *The Farmer's Year*, also still has a following in agricultural circles.

Although Henry Rider Haggard may be the best-known writer in the family, his youngest child Lilias Rider Haggard also carved a niche for herself as a writer on rural topics. Probably her best-known book, which she actually edited from the original author's penny exercise book of full of notes and musings, was *I Walked By Night: Being the Philosophy of the King of the Norfolk Poachers, Written by Himself.* It was the memoirs of a Norfolk countryman, mole-catcher, and not particularly lovable bigamist and rogue called Frederick (or Fred) Rolfe, who at the time was living in a cottage in Bungay. Lilias bought the manuscript, which chronicled the life and times of a member of what we'd now describe as the rural, criminal underclass.

Had he been around today, he'd have probably grown skunk cannabis in his attic-space but being a man of the late-nineteenth and early-twentieth centuries, Rolfe was a poacher. His Baldrick-like cunning plan was to leave his bicycle outside the front of his house at night, to fool the police into thinking he was at home, whereas he'd actually gone out the backdoor on another poaching trip.

It was possibly not the best way to establish an alibi as during his life Rolfe made at least thirty appearances before magistrates' courts, opting for short custodial prison sentences, often with hard labour, rather than pay a fine. His first conviction was when he was still a teenager, his last was when he was in his mid-sixties. Given his subsequent connection with Lilias Rider Haggard, there is also a certain irony that it was her father, Sir Henry, who was responsible for sending him to prison on several occasions.

Rolfe's ending is particularly pathetic as, finding himself at the age of seventy-seven in 1938, old, poor, crippled with arthritis, and facing another potentially very serious police investigation (possibly for a sexual assault) he opted to take his own life rather than spend the rest of it in prison or the municipal workhouse at Shipmeadow (on the Bungay to Beccles road). This might seem a drastic option but records suggest many elderly men in this era in similar straits to Rolfe, when there was no welfare state/social security net to fall back on, believed death by suicide was better than the dehumanising prospect of living out their days in the workhouse.

Rolfe chose to hang himself with a wire snare, the same type of snare he would have used in his poaching days to catch and strangle birds and small game. The story is Rolfe's body was discovered after a young boy returned home from school with a black eye. When asked by his mother what had happened, he said he'd taken a short cut through a stable-yard and been kicked in the face by Fred Rolfe – in other words he'd accidentally run into one of Rolfe's boots while the poacher was still twitching in his death throes.

Rolfe was buried in an unmarked grave in unconsecrated ground in Bungay Cemetery and is said to still haunt the place, as well he might as he was a firm believer in the weird. To quote his own words (and his spelling and grammar):

> The younger Generation do not beleve a lot that the old
> ones tell them these days. There used to be all sorts of
> legends in those days, gosts of all sorts, tales on
> Weanling Calves and shaggy Dogs that walked on the
> high way, and men riden about with no Heads on, and
> Panthom Carriages runing about the Cuntry side…

Sounds a lot like the Waveney valley even today if all the legends are to be believed. Incidentally the book *I Walked By Night* has never been out of print since it was first published in 1935. Lilias Rider Haggard paid Rolfe the princely sum of £20 for the manuscript.

QUITE
INTRIGUING
TOO

The Other Frederick Rolfe

Frederick Rolfe the poacher should not be confused with another Frederick Rolfe of the same era, namely the English writer and eccentric better known as Baron Corvo. The closest this Frederick Rolfe came to a brush with the law was when he was thrown out of a Roman Catholic seminary, bringing his hopes of becoming a priest to an end, because of his 'reputation as a pederast'. This Frederick Rolfe was buried in a clearly marked marble-fronted tomb in consecrated ground on the island cemetery of San Michele in the Venetian Lagoon.

SCULPTED FROM LIFE

The Rider Haggard family, including Sir Henry and Lilias, are buried at St Mary's Church, Ditchingham, but the highlight of any visit has to be the war memorial inside the church. Created by the distinguished sculptor Francis Derwent Wood in black marble and bronze, it is unlike anything you would normally expect to encounter in an out-of-the-way rural parish church.

Although too old to serve in the war, Derwent Wood made his own contribution to the war effort crafting and painting individual tin and copper facial masks for men who had been badly disfigured by bullet wounds and shrapnel. It may sound primitive to us now but in the days before reconstructive plastic surgery, these masks really did help men with hideous facial injuries to enjoy some semblance of a return to normal life. Indeed Derwent Wood's example was followed by other sculptors and military hospitals, with the authorities eventually creating a Facial Disfigurement Department, known to its patients as the Tin Noses Shop.

After the war, Derwent Wood went on to create some monumental public war memorials, including the highly controversial (so controversial that all photographs of it were banned and it was

The Ditchingham war memorial – speckling caused by disrespectful bats. Photo: Charles Christian.

hidden away from public view until 1992) *Canada's Golgotha* statue depicting a soldier who was allegedly crucified by German troops.

By comparison the Ditchingham memorial is a far more modest affair, the main feature being a full-size representation of a World War One soldier. Nothing unusual in this except such statues typically depict an idealised soldier. Ditchingham is different as it shows a real soldier, clearly drawn from life: it even shows his boots wrapped in non-standard Hessian sacking to provide some protection from the mud in the trenches. And, it shows a dead soldier, not one who is merely 'sleeping'. The soldier at Ditchingham has the sunken eyes of the recently dead and there is the gash of a shrapnel wound across his forehead.

Another unusual feature of the memorial, in the sense it is rarely seen on Great War memorials, is the list of the village's war dead also includes the name of a woman, Nurse Mary Rodwell, who died in 1915 when the hospital ship *HMHS Anglia* hit a mine in the English Channel while bringing wounded troops back from the Western Front.

Geldeston and the Beccles Road:
Black Dogs, Bigods and Vikings

The village of Geldeston has three claims to fame to earn it a place in this book.

The first is the Geld Stone, a large sandstone block that once stood at a crossroads and was, according to legend, the place where the Vikings would stand, when they had sailed up the Waveney from the coast, and demanded *gelt*, or gold, from the local population.

An eighteenth or nineteenth century-era antiquarian is thought to have devised this story as a handy explanation for the origins of the village's name where misplaced ingenuity (see also Harleston) overlook the historical evidence, including the fact the Vikings never actually travelled around villages demanding money. The money, called Danegeld, was collected by the local Saxon authorities and paid to the Vikings as bribes to stay away. It is now thought the village's name is a derivation of Gyldi's (a person's name) and *tun* (a settlement).

Sadly this is now all a little academic as the original geld stone, most likely a boundary or track marker, was moved into a private garden sometime around the beginning of the twentieth century and subsequently lost. Undaunted, to celebrate the Year 2000 Millennium, the village did splash out and buy itself a brand new stone, carved with the words *Geldeston 2000*.

The nearby village of Stockton also has its own geld stone, now known as the Stockton Stone. This is another of the Waveney valley's glacial erratics and it too was most likely once a boundary or track marker. You can still see the Stockton Stone, standing on a grassy bank at a lay-by on the A146 Beccles to Norwich road. The stone is said to have a curse on it and serious misfortune will befall anyone who tries to move it. It is unclear whether the story of the curse arose before or after an incident in the 1930s when one of the local council's workmen collapsed and died while the stone was being moved to its present location during road widening work.

But back to Geldeston for its second claim to fame, namely the legend that on certain nights of the year the lanes between the village and Bungay are haunted by a coach carrying Earl Hugh Bigod. The coach is driven by a headless coachman and pulled by four black horses, with large red eyes, flames coming from their mouths, and sparks flying from hooves. It is also said the coach is never both seen and heard. You either see it but don't hear it, or else hear it but don't see it.

East Anglia does seem to have a penchant for headless coachmen. On the anniversary of her death on May 19th, the ghost of Anne Boleyn, with her head in her lap, is said to arrive at her old home of Blickling Hall in a coach pulled by four headless horses and driven by a headless coachman. Meanwhile the ghost of her father, Sir Thomas Boleyn, is said to be doomed to walk the Earth for all eternity unless he can cross twelve Norfolk bridges between midnight and cockcrow on the same May night. This was Sir Thomas's divine punishment for doing nothing when both his daughter Anne and his son George were arrested, tried and subsequently beheaded on trumped-up charges of high treason, incest and adultery just so Henry VIII could marry his new mistress Jane Seymour. The catch is Sir Thomas has to cross the twelve bridges in a coach pulled by four headless horses and driven by a headless coachman.

There's even a ghostly coach driven by a headless coachman that crosses Bishop's Bridge in Norwich every Christmas Eve carrying 'Old Blunderhazard', an apparently cursed member of the Blennerhassett family. This manifestation manages the spectacular feat of being pulled by four headless horses which still have 'fire flashing from their nostrils'.

The third and final legend associated with Geldeston is that Black Shuck, although many locals call it the 'Hateful Thing', has been seen in and around the village on several occasions. The Waveney valley is undoubtedly Shuckland Central, with the excellent online resource *Hidden East Anglia* reporting over eighty different variants of the legend associated with the creature and 179 separate sightings. But just what is or was Black Shuck?

Is Shuck supernatural, such as a manifestation of the Devil or some other form of demonic entity? Alternatively, could Shuck be an abnormal but otherwise natural phenomenon, perhaps some kind of cryptid or remnant of an isolated pack of wild dogs or wolves? There is even a suggestion Shuck's origin may in some way be connected with the beliefs of the pagan Vikings, who once harassed the coasts and waterways of East Anglia and who honoured the god Odin, who was always accompanied by his two wolves Geri and Freki.

The search for an answer is further complicated by the fact there is little agreement as to what Black Shuck actually looks like or what is its true nature.

Descriptions of Black Shuck vary widely from just being a large black dog to a shaggy, rough-coated animal the size of a pony or calf. There is even wider discrepancy over Shuck's eyes. Does it have one large Cyclops-like eye in the centre of its forehead – or does it have two eyes? And are these eyes normal or 'saucer-sized, fiery, glowing eyes' that are red, yellow or green in colour?

Shuck also displays markedly different behavioural characteristics, sometimes malevolent, sometimes a *barghest*-like harbinger of death, yet at other times protective, looming out of the dark to protect a lonely traveller from footpads or what we'd now call muggers. Intriguingly, the only account of Black Shuck ever attacking and killing anyone is Fleming's *A Straunge and Terrible Wunder* from 1577.

It is also very interesting to read that of the 181 sightings of Shuck recorded by *Hidden East Anglia*, 142 of those took place during the twentieth century. In fact in the 1960s and 1970s alone there were as many sightings of Black Shuck as there were in total during the sixteenth to nineteenth centuries all combined.

So is Black Shuck becoming more active? Or do we have life imitating art so now, because the legend of Black Shuck is so well known, whenever anyone sees a big black dog running across a field in East Anglia, they automatically identify it as Black Shuck whereas in previous times they would have just seen a big black dog running loose? Folklorists call this 'ostension' – where ambiguous events are interpreted in terms of a legend or urban myth.

As already mentioned, the town of Bungay is never going to drop its attachment to the legend of Black Shuck but it also looks like remaining a permanent fixture of the wider East Anglian mythology, going by the widespread media coverage in 2014 of the discovery of the skeleton of a large Great Dane-type dog during an archaeological dig at Leiston Abbey on the Suffolk coast.

'Is this the skeleton of the legendary devil dog Black Shuck who terrorised 16th century East Anglia?' 'Hell Hound Found.' 'Black Shuck: Proof of Existence Finally Found?' And 'Bones of Hound from Hell Black Shuck Discovered' were just some of the sensationalist headlines that accompanied the discovery of the remains of some mediaeval abbot's prized and pampered pooch.

Chapter 10

Beccles:
Tower and Stone, Fish and Fire

As mentioned in Chapter 2, much of the history of the Waveney valley only makes sense when viewed in the context of what the terrain was like hundreds of years ago rather than it is now, and nowhere more so than the town of Beccles.

Located the southern shore of what was once the Waveney arm of the Great Estuary, Beccles was home to a small fishing port and, it is believed, the site of a watch tower located on high ground near where the parish church of St Michael now stands. In Roman times the occupants of the tower would have been looking for the boats of Saxon raiders, and then lighting a beacon to alert the residents of Bungay and beyond of the danger. Then, in Saxon times, the beacon would have been lit to warn of Viking raiders.

The location was precarious but the waters of the estuary were rich in fish, primarily herring, to the extent that by the early eleventh century the town was already paying a *tallage* (a form of tax) of 30,000 herrings a year and, by the time of the Domesday survey (completed 1086) this had increased to 60,000 herrings.

Beccles first appears in the written records in the mid-tenth century when King Edwy (see below) granted the manor to the abbey at St Edmund's Bury with the revenues being used to buy clothes and shoes for the monks.

For the next three centuries Beccles' wealth was primarily based on the herring fishery but, gradually, the Great Estuary began to silt up and the waters receded from the valley of the Waveney to create swathes of fen, salt-marsh and grazing pastures, while the new coastal towns of Great Yarmouth and Lowestoft emerged as the focal points for fishing.

THE SHORT BUT SCANDALOUS LIFE OF KING EDWY

King Edwy, also known as Eadwig or Edwin, the Saxon monarch who gifted the Beccles manors to the St Edmundsbury monks, occupied the throne of England for just four years. He first appears in the pages of history in accounts of his coronation in November 955.

Bored with listening to his advisers and church officials discussing politics, the young king – he was just fifteen years-old at the time – snuck off from the coronation feast and was next encountered 'minus his crown' in his private chamber 'cavorting' with two women: a noblewoman called Aethelgifu and her daughter Elgiva (or Aelfgifu).

It is not exactly clear from the accounts whether the mother was present merely to encourage Edwy and Elgiva to get to know each other better or whether they were enjoying a threesome. Certainly one report does describe him as having to be 'dislodged' from the bed where he was found lying between the two equally amorous women, while another says the king 'retreated to his chamber to debauch himself with two women, an indecent noblewoman and her daughter of ripe age'.

It's worth noting that at the time the king was regarded as being very good looking and often referred to as King Edwy the All-Fair, so we are looking at the equivalent of a Dark Age 'babe magnet' putting the sex into Wessex.

Unfortunately for Edwy, his absence from the feast was noticed and Dunstan, the Abbot of Glastonbury, was sent to look for him. After finding him in bed with the two women, Dunstan forcibly dragged him back to the feast. Then, with the royal crown once more properly on his head, Edwy was forced by Dunstan to publicly renounce Elgiva as a strumpet – which must have been as humiliating for the young king then as it would be for any teenager boy today being publicly chided for having an 'unsuitable' girlfriend.

Abbot Dunstan, who would later go on to become the Archbishop of Canterbury and subsequently be canonised as a saint, was by far the most influential cleric of his day. His reputation was also boosted by his two legendary encounters with the Devil.

According to one story, when Dunstan was still a monk, he was in his monastic cell playing his harp when the Devil came to tempt him. The Devil took the form of a pretty young girl but as 'she' danced around the cell, Dunstan spotted the cloven hoofs beneath her billowing skirts. Undaunted, Dunstan picked up a pair of blacksmith's tongs, he'd been heating on his forge (Dunstan was also an amateur blacksmith and silversmith) and pinched the Devil by the nose. As the rhyme tells it...

> St Dunstan, as the story goes,
> Once pull'd the Devil by the nose
> With red-hot tongs, which made him roar,
> That he was heard three miles or more.

In the second tale, the Devil had heard Dunstan was such a good farrier that his shoeing could make lame horses sound again. When the Devil asked Dunstan to re-shoe his own horse, Dunstan nailed a red-hot shoe to the Devil's own cloven foot. This caused Old Nick great pain but Dunstan only agreed to remove it after the Devil promised he would never enter a home that had a horseshoe nailed above its front door.

This is said to be the origin of the superstition about lucky horseshoes although I can find no agreement as to which way the horseshoe should be nailed. Some people say the open end should be at the top, so your luck will not escape, whereas others say it should be the opposite way around, so the luck will pour down on everyone who walks beneath it.

But back to King Edwy... Despite his run-in with Dunstan, Edwy subsequently married Elgiva and went on to be remarkably generous in terms of making donations and grants to the Church and other religious institutions, such as happened with Beccles.

Sadly relations between the king and his advisers rapidly deteriorated, with the crunch coming in 957 when the thanes (nobles) in the Northern provinces of Mercia and Northumbria switched allegiance to Edwy's younger brother Edgar and the kingdom was split in half. Two years later, in October 959, Edwy died at the still young age of nineteen and the kingdom of England was reunited under his brother Edgar. As for the cause of death, this has never been satisfactorily explained and its convenient timing has fueled the suspicion that Edwy was murdered by nobles belonging to his brother's party.

THE TOWER AND THE STONE

The most striking landmark in modern Beccles is the imposing parish church of St Michael the Archangel and its bell tower. Unusually for a Suffolk church (the only other one is St Andrew, Bramfield) the tower is separate from the body of the church – but why?

You often encounter one of two legends to explain this scenario. The first is it was the work of the Devil, attempting to disrupt the building of the church but instead of knocking over the tower, all he managed to do was push it away from the nave and the rest of the church. The second explanation is there were two patrons who funded the building of the church (usually two brothers or two sisters) but they couldn't agree on the design of the church, so one financed the construction of the body of the church and the other paid for the tower to be erected. Unfortunately it is only as the church is being completed they realise the tower has been built too far away to be connected to the rest of the church.

In the case of Beccles, there was no demonic intervention, nor sibling rivalry. The simple explanation is the original church, commenced in the mid-fourteenth century, comprised a chancel, nave, and porch but nothing else. Work on the bell tower did not start until about 150 years later in the early sixteenth century, when it was realised that if the tower were placed in its traditional position – at the west end of the chancel – it would be too near the edge of a bank (see below) to have adequate foundations to support its weight. Instead it was made a freestanding structure to the east of the church. There is a suggestion it was originally intended to have a spire as well but the Reformation brought construction work to halt.

Arguably the church's most significant contribution to the history of this country was the wedding, in 1749, of Catherine Suckling and the Reverend Edmund Nelson, a former curate of St Michael's. Horatio, the sixth of their eleven children, would grow up to become the English seafaring hero Admiral Lord Nelson.

And the stone? Lurking in the long grass at the back of St Michael's churchyard, on a steep bank known as The Cliff that the runs down to the Puddingmoor road, is a four-foot long slab of stone called the Puddingmoor Stone. It's yet another of the Waveney valley's glacial erratics and, depending upon which theory you care to believe, it is a marker stone from an old track, a fragment of the old watch tower that once stood near here, or even a sacred stone from pagan times that was at the heart of the original settlement.

THE GHOSTS OF ROOS HALL AND
THE THREE BURNING MEN

Roos Hall, a red-brick Tudor manor house (a private home, not open to the public, once owned by the Suckling family and apparently now owned by them again) on the outskirts of Beccles, is not only the most haunted location in the Waveney valley but also a contender for being one of the most haunted buildings in the entire country.

Every Christmas Eve a ghostly coach, driven by a headless coachman and pulled by four headless horses, arrives at the hall carrying the spectre of our friend from the last chapter, Old Blunderhazard, on his annual journey from the Blennerhassett family estate at Barsham, just a couple of miles from Beccles, to his property in Norwich and then back again before dawn.

Close by the hall is an ancient, twisted, gnarled old oak tree known as Nelson's Tree. Horatio is supposed to have played there as a child, the Suckling family connection again. Legend says the tree also served as a gallows and is now haunted by the ghosts of the men who were hanged there. It is even reported that on some nights you can still hear the rattling of chains, harking back to the time when the corpses of executed felons would be covered in tar then hung in chains from a gibbet as a warning to others.

The old oak tree is yet another location where reputedly if you walk around it in a widdershins (anticlockwise) direction six times (a mere half of the laps prescribed at Bungay) you will summon up the Devil. That said, an encounter with Old Nick might be preferable to an encounter with the Woman in White who can sometimes be seen standing beneath Nelson's Tree at night. It is not entirely clear whether she is the ghost of a witch who was hanged on the tree or a woman waiting for vengeance after her lover was wrongly executed there. Either way, the local legend says if she looks you straight in the eyes, you'll either go mad or die within the year.

The paranormal activity continues within Roos Hall. In one of the bedrooms is a fitted cupboard with what is claimed to be the imprint of the Devil's hoof burned into the brickwork. Perhaps someone once did raise more than they expected after walking around the oak six times? And there is also a haunted window that no matter how many times it is firmly closed and locked shut, will always be wide open again by the following morning.

Naturally the town of Beccles has many ghost stories but the most peculiar one is the legend of the three rat catchers, also known as the three burning men. The story goes that during medieval times, when the town was overrun with rats, three local men negotiated a deal with the town's corporation and guilds that they would rid the town of its rats in exchange for a large sum of money.

This they did by playing musical instruments, which so enchanted the rats that they followed the men out of the town, across the marshes, and down to the banks of the Waveney, where the rats all fell into the river and drowned. But, strangely, the three men never returned to claim their payment and in fact were never seen again.

Legend says the men sold their souls to a group of witches in exchange for the secret of enchanting the rats but, as so often happens with demonic pacts in folklore, there was a catch and as soon as the rats had all been swept away by the waters of the river, the three men were swallowed up by the fires of Hell. Their only respite from eternal damnation is once a year, on August 31st, their ghosts can be seen standing on the banks of the River Waveney.

This is a curious legend for Suffolk, as although there is little doubt reports of towns being overrun with rats and then succumbing to outbreaks of bubonic plague, such as the Black Death which devastated parts of East Anglia, would have lingered long in the collective memory, it also seems to share elements of the well-known (since at least the fourteenth century) German tale of the Pied Piper of Hamelin. But there is also an unpleasant incident in the town's actual historical record that may offer an explanation for the legend of the three burning men.

It was during the reign of Queen 'Bloody' Mary Tudor when an attempt to restore Roman Catholicism as the official religion of England saw the persecution of followers of the new Protestant faith. Suffolk was not immune from these 'Marian Persecutions' and on May 21st 1556, three men – Thomas Spicer, John Denny, and Edmund Poole – were all put to death by being burned at the stake in the old market square in Beccles. Perhaps this real-life tragedy became conflated with accounts of the Black Death and the story of the Pied Piper?

Although the River Waveney still has many miles to go before it flows into Breydon Water and enters the North Sea at Great Yarmouth, not far beyond Beccles the river leaves its valley confines and enters the sprawling, winding network of waterways that is the Norfolk Broads – and the area that was once the Great Estuary of Roman and Saxon times. In the next chapter we'll continue our journey to the sea – and consider whether this is really journey's end?

QUITE INTRIGUING TOO

The Blennerhassett Family

The Blennerhassett family – the family of 'Old Blunderhazard' – have their origins in twelfth century Cumbria. However in the early fifteenth century part of the family relocated to East Anglia, while a century later another branch of the family settled in County Kerry, Ireland. Then, two hundred years later another branch of the family, headed by Harman Blennerhassett, settled in North

America – Blennerhassett Island on the Ohio river takes its name from the family.

Technically the male line of the family is now extinct in Britain but the name lives on in family connections and in other countries. In Ireland for example, the late John Blennerhassett was actively involved in politics and a member of the Dáil Éireann (Irish parliament) until 1982, while as long ago as 1912, the family tree was dropped from *Burke's Landed Gentry* because it had grown so complicated. In fact the situation was summed up as long ago as the late seventeenth century when John 'Black Jack' Blennerhassett (possibly the model for Old Blunderhazard) commented:

> Show me the country, place, or spot of ground, where
> 'Hassetts or their allies are not found.

There is also an intriguing connection between the Blennerhassett's and the poet John Skelton we encountered in Diss. One of Skelton's poems is titled *To Mistress Jane Blennerhasset* and runs:

> When though my pen wax faint,
> And hath small lust to paint?
> Yet shall there no restraint
> Cause me to cease,
> Among this press,
> For to increase
> Your goodly name.

Who was Jane Blennerhasset (or Blennerhassett)? It is possible she was a cousin or ancestor of John Skelton, as a Jane de Skelton married Ralph de Blenerhaysett sometime around the year 1400 and they were the branch of the family who moved from Cumbria to East Anglia, settling at Barsham Hall, near Beccles, and Frenze Hall, just outside Diss.

CHAPTER 11

JOURNEY'S END – OR JOURNEY'S BEGINNING?

We're now heading for the final leg of our journey from Beccles to the East Coast – but it could be argued the coast is actually where it all begins. To understand this apparent contradiction, we will be delving into both ancient history and Earth Mysteries but before we do so, we need to visit the church of St Mary the Virgin on the outskirts of the village of Burgh St Peter, just a few miles downriver from Beccles.

The Burgh church is famous for three things. The first is its redbrick five-stage square tower, which looks a little like a wedding cake but was actually inspired by the design of the Ancient Mesopotamian ziggurats. Apparently local residents used to tell people taking boating holidays on the Norfolk Broads that the tower could be extended and contracted like a telescope, and was lowered during the winter and only raised again during the summer to provide a handy landmark for visitors.

The second claim to fame is that from the mid-eighteenth to late-nineteenth centuries, five successive generations of the same family – the Boycotts – were rectors of this church. They are all buried in the first stage of the tower, which serves as a family mausoleum.

The family is now best known for the son, Captain Charles Boycott, who did not take holy orders but instead became the infamous land agent in Ireland. We encountered Captain Boycott at Flixton Hall earlier in this book. Captain Boycott was also buried in the family mausoleum, the funeral service being conducted by his nephew Arthur. However Captain Boycott's widow Annie was subsequently sued over the funeral expenses, along with other debts, and had to

St Mary's at Burgh St Peter, the ziggurat on the Waveney.
Photo: Charles Christian.

sell some of her assets. (Where there's a will, there's always a family and often a war.)

And then we have the church's third claim to fame: its ghost. Or should that be a doomed spirit trapped for all eternity in a churchyard porch?

This is an intriguing story as the legend holds that the church's original builder, a certain Adam Morland, sold his soul to the Devil in exchange for knowledge and wisdom on how to complete the construction of the building. When he died – it was on May 2nd – he was buried within the church itself, so the Devil could not claim his soul. But his spirit is now trapped within the building. Because he sold his soul, his spirit cannot rise up to Heaven but if it strays outside the church, it will be dragged away to Hell.

So now, once a year, every May 2nd, the builder's ghost – reduced to a skeleton in a raggedy shroud – can be seen flitting around the church porch, which is on holy ground and therefore protected, peering out to see if the Devil has finally given up waiting to enforce the demonic pact the builder so foolishly signed all those centuries ago. An added irony is the church he sold his soul to build was subsequently transformed out of all recognition long after his death by the Boycotts, who were responsible for erecting the ziggurat-like tower. (See also Quite Intriguing Too: More Ghosts of the Norfolk Broads.)

Following the ley-line to Hopton-on-Sea

Shortly beyond the village of Burgh St Peter, the River Waveney halts its west-to-east flow, turns back on itself in a north-westerly direction for a few miles then twists to the north-east to join the River Yare at the entrance to Breydon Water before finally flowing into the North Sea at Great Yarmouth.

As mentioned at the beginning of the book, confused novice boaters on the Norfolk Broads could be forgiven for thinking the Waveney flows directly towards Oulton Broad, Lake Lothing and the sea at Lowestoft thanks to a one-mile stretch of water called the Oulton Dyke.

So which arm should we follow? The answer is neither because, to pick up on a point also mentioned at the outset, for much of its path the Waveney valley coincides with the route of a ley-line. This is the Great St Michael and St Mary Alignment, probably the most famous ley-line in the world, and we will now follow this to the coast.

Now I'll admit that for many people, ley-lines are a Marmite concept they either love or hate and which can be explained in one of three different ways namely: they are historical, mystical or purely coincidental phenomena.

Another way of looking at ley-lines is to see them as occupying the liminal space between legitimate landscape archaeology, the concept of the ritual (or ceremonial/mythical) landscape, and the pseudoscience (or alternative archaeology) of Earth Mysteries. And see Appendix 1: All You Ever Wanted to Know About Ley-Lines But Were Afraid to Ask.

The 350-mile long St Michael and St Mary Alignment (also called the Atlantis Ley) runs across England in a orthenast to southwesterly-direction ending at Land's End. There is a suggestion it stretches even farther beyond, out into the waters of the Atlantic to the lost kingdom of Lyonesse of Celtic and Arthurian legend, of which only the Scilly Isles still remain above the surface today. On its way west, it passes through Bury St Edmunds Cathedral and the Home Counties before running on across over a dozen or more significant historical and archaeological sites including the Avebury henge complex, Glastonbury Tor and St Michael's Mount.

Our focus is on the eastern end of the alignment, where it enters the territory covered by this book, embracing The Mere at Diss, the mysterious stone in Harleston, the hill on which the parish church of Saint Mary the Virgin, Denton, is located (which is about two miles away from where yours sincerely wrote this book), the ruins of Bungay Castle, and the still-thriving Somerleyton Hall estate, before finally running into the North Sea at Hopton-on-Sea, which is almost the most easterly point on the East Anglian coastline. I also suggested you keep a note of the number of churches dedicated either to the Archangel Michael or the Virgin Mary.

There are St Michaels at Occold, near Eye, South Elmhall, Broome, Geldeston, Beccles, and Oulton, near Lowestoft; but when it comes to St Marys, the number is truly enormous. The stretch of the ley-line from Bury St Edmunds to Diss includes churches dedicated to the Virgin Mary at Pakenham, Ixworth, Langham, Waltham le Willows, both Rickinghall Superior and Rickinghall Inferior, Hinderclay, Redgrave, Wortham, Mellis, and Burgate, as well as Bury St Edmunds itself. Then there are churches dedicated to St Mary at Diss, Gissing, Pulham St Mary, Brome, Yaxley, Thorpe Parva (now a sparse ruin), Tivetshall St Mary (rather more substantial ruins),

Thorpe Parva tower.
Photo: Charles Christian.

Redenhall/Harleston, Denton, Homersfield, Bungay, Ditchingham, Ellingham, Gillingham, Aldeby, Ashby, Haddiscoe, Somerleyton and Blundeston.

Blundeston, incidentally, was the birthplace of Charles Dickens' fictional character David Copperfield, while Haddiscoe was the location of the only Knights Templar preceptory in Norfolk. As for Somerleyton Hall, possibly the weirdest event in its history was when the lake was used by Sir Christopher Cockerell, the inventor of the hovercraft, to carry out his early experiments in the 1950s. Actually that is not quite true as there is a legend that in 'olden days' Somerleyton was once the hunting area of a giant. The giant apparently stumbled across a plot to murder him, so struck first and killed the would-be assassin. The would-be assassin's blood is now said to rain down from the sky in the anniversary of the killing every November 19th.

Incidentally, the latter section of the St Michael and St Mary Alignment, along the Waveney valley to the coast, also coincides with part of the newly-established *Via Beata* long-distance Christian pilgrimage route across the UK at its widest point from Lowestoft in East Anglia to St Davids in West Wales.

But any discussion of the route of the Alignment does raise one obvious question, namely why does it abruptly end at Hopton-on-Sea of all places? Arguably, the only significant feature there is the Potters Resort holiday camp, home of the World Indoors Bowls Championships. Even Hopton's church is not dedicated to St Michael or St Mary but to St Margaret. (There is an alternative suggestion it actually ends at the village of Ormesby St Michael, a few miles north of Great Yarmouth but personally I'm not convinced by this.)

DOGGERLAND, THE ICE AGES AND TIN

For an explanation, we need to go a long way back, to a time when England was still joined to Continental Europe. The connection was not at the closest point today the Straits of Dover, which has actually been a sea channel between England and France for nearly half-a-million years, but a now lost landmass called Doggerland (derived from the Dogger Bank), that sat between East Anglia and what is now the Netherlands, northwest Germany, and Denmark.

When the last Ice Age descended on the northern Hemisphere, temperatures plummeted to such a point that most of northern Europe, including the British Isles was abandoned as people moved south towards the Mediterranean and warmer climates. (Ice Age should officially read glacial period – technically we are now living in the Holocene interglacial period although it will probably be another 50,000 years before another ice age comes along, so no need to panic-buy bread and rolls of toilet paper at the supermarket, at least not just yet)

Incredibly, the ice sheet covering Europe during the last Ice Age was in some parts between three to four kilometres (or 2.0–2.5 miles) thick. Quick translation: that's snow and ice so deep that 70 Nelson's Columns stacked on top of each other would not break the surface. Even in parts not covered by ice, the countryside would have been bitterly cold and inhospitable tundra. Nevertheless eventually the climate did begin to improve and by 15,500–14,000 years ago people began moving back into northern France, Belgium, northwest Germany, and the southern part of the British Isles. (There would still be glaciers in the north of Scotland until about 10,000 years ago.)

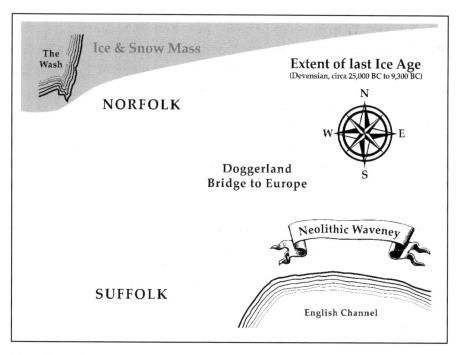

For those heading for Britain, the entry point was Doggerland and the most attractive part of the country – the part that had escaped the ice sheet – was broadly England south of a line between the Wash in the east and the Bristol Channel in the west. (Earlier ice ages extended further south, which explains the presence of those many glacial erratics.)

Initially these visitors to southern England would have been summer migrants, returning to southern parts of Europe with the arrival of winter but, in due course, many settled here, making it their permanent home. A home made all the more permanent when rising sea levels turned Doggerland into, firstly, a chain of islands before ultimately swallowing the remaining landmass beneath the waves.

The final disappearance of Doggerland, sometimes romantically called the British Atlantis, was between 5,000–4,700 BC. But don't be fooled by the Atlantis allusion, for Doggerland was no classical civilisation with glittering cities of white marble and people in togas. Instead, it was the domain of nomadic tribes of hunter-gathers whose technology reflected the prevailing Mesolithic-Neolithic culture of worked flints, and harpoons and fishing barbs carved from antlers. But let's get back to the Waveney valley...

For the first visitors making their way to post-Ice Age England, not only would the Norfolk/Suffolk coastline have been the obvious point of entry but also progressing across the countryside, steering clear of the terrain still recovering from the ice sheet, would have taken them along the Waveney valley and then in a south-westerly direction. In other words they would have been following the route of what would become known as the St Michael and St Mary Alignment.

Of course it is often said that ley-lines don't actually exist except in theory but it is worth noting that two historical, possibly dating back to Neolithic times, long-distance trackways do actually follow the St Michael and St Mary Alignment for much of their way. Used by traders and drovers for thousands of years, these two routes – The Ridgeway and the Icknield Way – also pass close by many of the same ancient sites as the ley-lines.

The westerly of the two, The Ridgeway, follows the line of the Chilterns and the Wessex Downs, to the Avebury Henge. From there on there is some debate as to whether it continued south to terminate at the Dorset coast or south-westerly to Land's End. The easterly end of The Ridgeway is the starting point for the Icknield Way, which runs east across the northern Home Counties into East Anglia, where it peters out at Knettishall Heath, midway between the Norfolk towns of Thetford and Diss.

Once again there is some debate where it ultimately terminates. One suggestion is it turned northwards towards The Wash, following what is now known as the Peddars Way long distance footpath (total distance 49 miles/79 km) that ends at Holme-next-the-Sea (near Hunstanton) on the north Norfolk coast, close to the Bronze Age timber circle site of Seahenge. In prehistoric times, the area west of the Wash (including the Fens of Cambridgeshire and Lincolnshire) would have been an unattractive mix of rivers, marshes and tidal mudflats (as indeed it remained until the medieval period) making it impassable to most travellers.

Another suggestion is its destination was the homeland of the Celtic Iceni tribe (there is an argument that the name Icknield is derived from Iceni) and what would later become the Roman-British town of *Venta Icenorum.*

There is a third suggestion that it would have continued in a north-easterly direction towards the Norfolk-Suffolk coast midway between what is now Great Yarmouth and Lowestoft. In other words Hopton-on-Sea, again, the one-time gateway to and from Doggerland. (Incidentally, the Norfolk Coast Path, a long-distance walking trail, runs all the way around the Norfolk Coast from Holme-next-the-Sea to Hopton-on-Sea, a total distance of 84 miles/135 km.)

While these south-westerly heading trackways would have clearly made sense to the earliest post-Ice Age visitors to these shores, because they formed the simplest and most direct migration route, why were they apparently still in use thousands of years later?

The answer lay in two discoveries.

The first was that by adding tin to copper (the tin element comprises between ten and twenty percent) you could create the alloy bronze, which is substantially harder than pure copper.

The second was the discovery of tin in Cornwall, where large-scale mining started in around 2,100 BC, if not earlier.

The net result was this Cornish tin fueled the Bronze Age not just in Ancient Britain but also across Western Europe. And the way tin merchants and traders found their way across England to and from the mines, in the days long before any roads were constructed, never mind maps, signposts, compasses, and satnav, was to follow the ancient trackways.

Cornwall and its tin mines was the economic powerhouse of the Bronze Age in England, in the same way the factories and mills of the great Northern, Midlands and Scottish cities would become the powerhouses of the British Empire during the Industrial Revolution.

In this context, the St Michael and St Mary Alignment, running across the country in a straight line from the tin mines of Cornwall to the

Norfolk Coast, was the Bronze Age equivalent of the Great North Road (now A1) and the network of canals and railway lines snaking north across the country from London to the industrial heartlands of the North.

QUITE INTRIGUING TOO

More Ghosts of the Norfolk Broads

Strictly speaking the main swathe of the Norfolk Broads is outside the scope of this book, which means we'll not be looking at the many ghost stories associated with the Broads, such as the well-known tale of the Phantom Drummer of Hickling Broad – the shade of a Napoleonic Wars-era soldier who used to skate across the frozen water to meet the girl he was courting... that was until the day the ice broke and he drowned. However a warning should be given about a book called *Ghosts of the Broads* by Charles Sampson. This contains twenty-five blood-curdling stories of ghosts, gouls and a surprising number of fiery-eyed animated skeletons. The only problem is while some are based around long-standing legends, many of the stories are entirely fake and were concocted by Sampson.

The background is Charles Sampson was a Harley Street physician who used to take boating holidays on the Norfolk Broads. In the late 1920s he wrote a series of short ghost stories for *The Yachtsman* magazine, which were later reissued in 1931 as a collection called *Ghosts of the Broads* and, among other things, distributed to customers of Broads yacht and motor-cruiser hire companies. Sampson intended them to be ripping yarns to thrill holidaymakers taking boating holidays and you can imagine they were very effective, being read by candlelight in a boat moored up against the crumbling ruins of an old church tower or windmill.

Sampson added to the effectiveness of these stories by reporting supposed eyewitness accounts and quoting various august-sounding journals and Latin chronicles as references. But almost all the references mentioned were entirely fictional, as were the

eyewitnesses. The next major development took place over forty years later when a new edition of *Ghosts of the Broads* was published in 1973. Unfortunately somewhere along the way the editors of the new edition neglected to make clear this was fiction, so for many years the book was treated as a ghost-hunting 'bible' by local paranormal investigation groups who 'spent many long (and futile) hours waiting in cold, dark and uncomfortable locations hoping to see at least one of the apparitions mentioned...' *Ghosts of the Broads* is still in print and is still a work of fiction.

Part Two: Earth Mysteries

The Old Minster & Ley-Lines

CHAPTER 12

THE MYSTERIOUS OLD MINSTER

In this book we have looked at many legends and mysteries but before we head into the latter stages of our journey, here is one final mystery – or coincidence – which links the St Michael and St Mary Alignment and the Old Minster at South Elmham, the building Sir Nikolaus Pevsner described as 'mysterious in purpose and also in date and plan'.

The key to any good mystery is a series of puzzles for which there are no good answers. Nowhere in the east of England is this more apparent than with the mystery of the Old Minster. Today it is just a pile of ruinous stonework, albeit ruinous stonework with a distinctly mysterious if not ominous presence. In fact it has been described as 'one of the most the romantic and enigmatic ruins in England' although others have commented that it seems unnaturally silent with not even birdsong being heard there.

Set within a small wood, within a small field in an obscure corner of the Suffolk countryside on the southern side of the Waveney valley, the site continues to raise more questions than it answers: Who built the present building? When was it built? What was its purpose? Why was it built facing in the wrong direction? Given its relativrely obscure location, why was this site chosen? What previously occupied this site?

And how far back in time does the history of this site extend? Are we talking Christian or Pagan? Pre-Christian or prehistoric? Norman or Saxon? Romano-British or Celtic? Or even earlier, to a time of myths and legends?

LET'S START WITH WHAT WE DO KNOW ABOUT THE OLD MINSTER...

At some point towards the end of the eleventh century, perhaps as late as 1096 to 1100, the Norman prelate Herbert de Losinga, the first Bishop of Norwich and the founder of Norwich Cathedral, acquired the manor of South Elmham and established an episcopal chapel there, close by the location of his summer retreat and Bishop's Palace at South Elmham Hall. We also know that by the middle-third of the fourteenth century the site had been abandoned and was falling into decay, with some of its dressed stonework being stolen and reused elsewhere, including the nearby churches of St Michael South Elmham and St Peter South Elmham.

What we also know is that during pagan Saxon times (specifically the fifth and sixth centuries) the land surrounding the Old Minster was used for burials. Perhaps more significantly, we know both the Old Minster and the Saxon cemetery were surrounded by the ditch and ramparts of a Roman fort, generally agreed to have been established in the months after the defeat of Boudicca's revolt in the years 60 and 61.

Boudicca (or Boadicea as she was called up until the 1950s) was the queen of the Celtic Iceni tribe, and the Waveney valley was not only part of their homeland but also the location of one of their most important ceremonial sites. Archaeological excavations suggest the nearby Flixton gravel terraces were a centre of ritual ceremony and reverence for the dead for more than 3,000 years from 2,500 BC in the Bronze Age to AD 600 in the pagan Saxon era. The Flixton site has also revealed early Neolithic worked flints and late Neolithic pottery shards.

We have no official record or explanation for the reason why the Old Minster was abandoned although given its mid-fourteenth century date the most likely explanation is the Black Death outbreak of plague, which struck during 1348–49 and briefly returned in 1361–62. Estimates vary but the old idea that it killed about one-third of the population has been revised upwards to between forty to sixty percent of the population in England. The latter figure would amount to something in the region of 3,750,000 deaths out of a total population of just six million.

Recent research also suggests fatalities may have been as high as sixty-five percent in East Anglia, and that the clergy generally suffered a higher than average death rate. This was presumably because they were in the front line and exposed to infection while administering to the sick, hearing their final confessions, being called to perform the Last Rites for the dying and dead, and organising burials. Certainly the Ordination Registers of the time shows the Church engaged in an unprecedented recruitment and ordination campaign during the plague years.

In the circumstances of 'the Great Mortality' as it was also known – in reality a catastrophic near-extinction event of apocalyptic proportions in the east of England, the dramatic reduction in congregation numbers and available clergy resulted in not just the Old Minster but also many other churches becoming redundant and abandoned. And then the entire world was turned upside down.

The Black Death hastened the end of the Feudal System by the early fifteenth century. Then came the religious upheavals of the Reformation and counter-Reformation of the sixteenth century, the political upheavals and civil wars of the seventeenth century, the Industrial Revolution of the eighteenth and early nineteenth century, with the wholesale migration of rural populations to the cities, and finally, in the twentieth century, the mechanisation of farming. In the circumstances it is hardly surprising places such as the Old Minster were forgotten as the people who knew their significance either died or moved away.

WHAT WE DON'T KNOW ABOUT THE OLD MINSTER

Those are the few uncontentious facts but they only address part of the story.

For example, if the Old Minister was only intended to be an episcopal chapel, why did Bishop de Losinga need such a large building? The Old Minster would have been ninety feet long and twenty-seven feet wide, with walls nearly five feet thick in places. In contrast to the

nearby parish church of All Saints South Elmham is just forty-eight feet long.

So was the Old Minster a new build by Herbert de Losinga or did he utilise and adapt an older building that was already on the site? Which in turn prompts the question: what was that earlier building?

Another mystery is why did a go-ahead, go-getting Norman prelate like de Losinga, who had already moved the episcopal see from Thetford to Norwich, opt for a church with what for even those times was a distinctly anachronistic, antiquated design?

By the tenth century (if not before) English churches had already settled down to their current layout of a rectangular chancel at the eastern end (the chancel is the sacred part that was the domain of the priests and houses the altar) and a larger (also rectangular) nave where the congregation stood. Seating did not become a feature of English churches until the thirteenth and fourteenth centuries. In addition, the main entry to the church would have been through a south-facing side door and porch.

But this is not the layout of the Old Minster. Instead, the South Elmham ruins indicate a building that had an entrance to the west, a curved or *apsidal* chancel at the east, and a central section of the church split between a nave and a *narthex*.

A narthex is a feature of early Christian churches where people who were excluded from services would stand, perhaps because they were penitents, unbaptised, or otherwise not full members of the congregation. In some churches, a large curtain would be drawn across the divide between the nave and the narthex at certain points during the service (such as the consecration and celebration of the Mass) so the excluded could not even see what was taking taking place.

By Bishop de Losinga's time the requirement to exclude some people from services had been removed, so for him to have included one in his chapel would have been an anachronism. All of which supports the theory that the South Elmham site was an existing, older building that the Bishop repurposed and, presumably, rebuilt. But how old was the original building, if it was not built by de Losinga?

Because there is very little dressed stonework remaining (and some of the pieces that were found have subsequently been identified as reworked Saxon grave slab fragments) all we are left with is the flintwork – which is almost impossible to accurately date and could have been erected in 1050, 950, 850, 750 or even 650 – and the archaic architecture.

At least one source has suggested the Old Minster's thick walls indicate it was constructed with a view to making it a place of refuge and defence in the event of a Viking raid: the first Viking raids into East Anglia were around 841.

But other aspects of the architecture, including the single-splay windows, the western doorway, the narthex, and the curved chancel, have more in common with the earliest Christian churches of the Saxon era in England. These include the old church of St Mary (also known as Bassa's Church, after the priest who had it built) at Reculver in Kent, and the three churches of St Mary, St Pancras, and SS Peter and Paul in Canterbury, also in Kent.

All date back to the mid-seventh century and, as one of the earliest bishops in East Anglia was Bishop Bertgils Boniface – described by the chronicler and church historian the Venerable St Bede, writing just a generation later, as a 'Kentish man' – there is a possibility that he may have been influential in the design of the Old Minster following those of the churches he was already familiar with in Kent.

We therefore find a date for the Old Minster ranging back from Bishop de Losinga in 1100 to as early as Bishop Boniface in 660. And, by way of adding a further permutation to contend with, it is most likely the original building at South Elmham was constructed of timber and that its later replacement, built of stone, deliberately replicated its now obsolete design.

THE OLD MINSTER – CHAPEL OR CATHEDRAL?

So much for the bricks and mortar of the Old Minster – or at least the flints and stonework – but what was its purpose? To set this into some kind of context, we first need to have a look at the evolution and history of Christianity in England in general and East Anglia in particular.

The first evidence of Christianity in what was then the Roman Empire's province of Britannia can be dated back to AD 180 (according to Bede) and arrived by boat with merchants travelling from other parts of the Empire. Probably to buy tin in Cornwall at the far western end of the St Michael and St Mary ley-line.

We can discount, as medieval PR spin by the monks of Glastonbury in the twelfth century, the story that Joseph of Arimathea – the man who provided the tomb for Christ's burial – was responsible for bringing Christianity to Britain (along with the legendary Holy Grail used at the Last Supper) and establishing Glastonbury Abbey. The medieval monks of Glastonbury also found the grave of King Arthur and Queen Guinevere in the abbey grounds in 1191. This was highly convenient as it boosted pilgrimage traffic, which had been falling, and helped raise funds to repair the abbey.

There is an alternative founding myth that the first Christian bishop of Roman Britain was St Aristobulus, an assistant to St Andrew, one of the twelve disciples, and a companion of St Paul. According to the legend, St Aristobulus travelled to Britain as a missionary, preached here and subsequently died here in around AD 56. The pilgrimage traffic-hungry monks at Glastonbury also claimed St Aristobulus founded their abbey and died there.

Regardless of its origins, Christianity was still a fringe cult in Britain and as late as 304, Romano-British Christians, such as St Alban, were being martyred for their beliefs. The game-changing event was the Edict of Milan in 313, when the Emperor Constantine the Great declared religious tolerance for Christians within the Roman Empire. And, the following year, three British bishops were in France (or Gaul as it was then called) representing the dioceses of London, York, and Lincoln (or possibly Colchester) at the Council of Arles. That said, the early Christian church in Britain was not exactly a thriving community as it's reported the delegation to the Council of Rimini in 353 had to beg for financial assistance from fellow delegates to fund their journey home.

While many Christian meetings and religious ceremonies still took place in private houses or repurposed civic buildings (including former pagan temples), the late Romano-British period also saw the construction of the first churches. Most of these have vanished without a trace although remains of buildings have been found in Lincoln, Canterbury, and Colchester. It was during this period (the fourth century) that Britain even managed to become home to one of the earlier heresies to dog the Christian church, namely Pelagianism. Fortunately we have no need to explore this particular flavour of heresy.

Unfortunately the worsening geopolitical situation in continental Europe saw the withdrawal of most of the Roman legions from Britannia in 407, with the end of Roman Britain coming three years later in 410 when the Emperor Honorius told the British to 'look to their own defences'.

Facing raids from the Angles and Saxons in the South and East, and the Picts and Scots in the North and west, the Christian settlements of England found themselves increasingly threatened by pagan invaders. The situation became so bad that by the latter part of the fifth century and the start of the sixth century Saxon paganism had become the dominant spiritual force across England. It destroyed organised Christian religion and the ecclesiastical institutions that supported it, and drove its adherents underground or else into Celtic/Gaelic fringes of Cornwall, Wales, Scotland, and Ireland.

There, cut off from the centre of Christianity in Rome, the church developed its own insular form of faith, generally known as Celtic Christianity. One of the biggest differences with the Roman church was the calculation of when Easter fell, however at the time another bone of contention was the correct way in which to shave a tonsure. Yes, the two sides could not agree on fashions for priestly haircuts.

The next major development came in 595 when Pope Gregory (later St Gregory the Great) in Rome appointed Augustine (later the first Archbishop of Canterbury and, later still, St Augustine) to lead a mission to convert the Anglo-Saxons of England to Christianity.

The popular story says Gregory was inspired to launch the mission after encountering some fair-haired, fair-skinned youths for sale in Rome's slave market. Upon being told they were Angles, he replied 'Not Angles but angels.' History would suggest that although Gregory took notice of them, he was not sufficiently concerned about the plight of these slaves to buy them so he could set them free.

Augustine enjoyed some success, converting the Kingdom of Kent and also establishing bishoprics in London and Rochester but seventh century Britain was a heptarchy of separate kingdoms, not just Kent but also Essex, Sussex, Wessex, Mercia, Northumbria, and East Anglia – and they all had to be converted separately.

In the Kingdom of East Anglia, the leading missionary was Felix of Burgundy (later St Felix) who assisted the then king Sigeberht (or Sigbert), a member of the Saxon Wuffinga royal dynasty, to establish Christianity among its population of the 'North Folk' and the 'South Folk'. Felix also became the first Bishop of East Anglia, establishing his episcopal see (or bishopric) at a place called Dommoc (or Domnoc or Dunmoc, more about its location later) in around 630. Just over forty years later in 672–3, the then Archbishop of Canterbury (later

St Theodore of Tarsus) split the East Anglian diocese into two with the establishment of the new bishopric of Elmham (or Helmham, much, much more about its location later.)

And then everyone lived happily ever after. Except they didn't because in the middle of the ninth century, the Vikings started regularly invading the area, culminating in the invasion by the Great Heathen Army, who we encountered in an earlier chapter, which in 869–70 crushed the kingdom of East Anglia and executed its last Christian monarch, King Edmund.

The year 870 also saw accounts of the two dioceses of Dommoc and Elmham vanish from the ecclesiastical records, and there is a good deal of evidence to suggest that Hunbeorht (or Humbertus), the last Bishop of Elmham, suffered the same fate as King Edmund. The village of Homersfield, not far from the Old Minister probably named after this unfortunate prelate.

Because the mid-ninth century Viking invasion almost wiped out Christianity in East Anglia, there are even fewer monastic records than usual for this part of the country during the so-called Dark Ages. In fact after 870 there is a gap in the episcopal records until 955 when we hear of the two dioceses being combined and Bishop Eadwulf being consecrated the Bishop of Elmham. The line of Elmham bishops continued until after the Norman Conquest in 1066 but four years later the last Saxon Bishop of Elmham, Aethelmaer, was deposed and his incoming Norman replacement Bishop Herfast set about transferring the episcopal see from Elmham to Thetford.

Twenty years later, in 1094, it was all change again when the new Bishop of Thetford, Herbert de Losinga, transferred the East Anglian see again, this time to Norwich, where it has remained ever since. This also neatly brings us back to where we started this chapter with Bishop de Losinga then going on to acquire the South Elmham manor and establish an episcopal chapel at the Old Minster.

But, all of this begs one important question: where was this place called Elmham that was the second diocese of East Anglia during the Saxon period up until 870? The problem here is there are two Elmhams in East Anglia: 'our' one at South Elmham in Suffolk and the other one we briefly mentioned earlier, North Elmham, in mid-Norfolk, about five miles north of town of East Dereham.

A Tale of Two Elmhams

There is little doubt from historical records, charters, and archaeology that when Christianity was being re-established in East Anglia in 955, following the disruption of the Viking era, the newly combined diocese was based not at South Elmham but at North Elmham. Not least because as part of the re-Christianisation of East Anglia, in 960 the Bishop of London had also established a bishopric *'Hoxne at mi bishoperiche'* at the Suffolk town of Hoxne (the site of King Edmund's martyrdom almost a century earlier) and it would have made no sense to have one bishopric at Hoxne and another less than ten miles away at South Elmham. The Hoxne bishopric ended around the time of the Norman Conquest in 1066, shortly before the Elmham see moved to Thetford.

Excavations of the ruins of the old private episcopal chapel at North Elmham, built sometime between 1091 and 1119 by Herbert de Losinga, have uncovered the foundations of three earlier timber structures built on the same site. At least one of them was the late Saxon cathedral, which would have been abandoned when the see transferred to Thetford in 1071. One of the other timber buildings may have been an earlier version of the cathedral that was burned by the Viking leader Sweyn Forkbeard who led his army through Norfolk in 1004. This is the same Sweyn Forkbeard who, according to legend, would be stabbed to death by the ghost of King Edmund.

The North Elmham excavations also suggest the episcopal chapel Bishop de Losinga had constructed was, for its time, a very modern ecclesiastical building, which is in stark contrast to the Old Minster at South Elmham. In describing the North Elmham chapel, English Heritage note that 'the rather eccentric design of the chapel reflects that of much grander European churches of the period', which certainly sounds more like something that would have appealed to the thoroughly modern prelate Herbert de Losinga.

AND A TALE OF TWO DOMMOCS

By way of an added distraction, before we can establish which Elmham was the original, pre-Viking incursion Elmham, we first need to work out where the original Saxon bishopric of Dommoc was located. There is a popular assumption that Dommoc was Dunwich on the Suffolk coast but was it?

Although Dunwich has been frequently described as the lost capital of East Anglia, this seems to be based on little more than romantic wishful thinking rather than any hard historical evidence. The archaeology is even harder to come by as almost all the town has long since fallen into the sea and even the ruins have been washed away.

Rather more importantly, its glory days were not in the Saxon era but in the years after the Norman Conquest during the twelfth and thirteenth centuries, when Dunwich was one of the ten largest cities in England and a major international seaport, with a shipping trade comparable with that of London. And by this time the East Anglian bishopric had long since been unified and moved to Norwich.

Being a wealthy city, Dunwich had a large ecclesiastical presence with apparently as many as eighteen churches, chapels, and monasteries at its height, including a Franciscan (Greyfriars) priory, a Dominican (Blackfriars) priory, and a Knights Templar preceptory. But there is no record of a cathedral building or even a building known as the site of the 'Old Cathedral'.

There is however a second and rather more convincing candidate for the location of Dommoc and that is the old Roman-era Saxon Shore fort of Walton Castle, near what is now the coastal town of Felixstowe, which in turn was named after St Felix. The records say the East Anglian monarch King Sigeberht granted Bishop Felix a coastal site at which to base his new diocese. Now the choice of an old military fort for an ecclesiastical establishment might seem somewhat irreconcilable but in the early says of English Christianity, this was a common model.

In Kent, the local king gave the old Roman fort at Reculver to the priest Bassa so he could build his church there. In Essex, St Cedd was given royal encouragement to set up his mission at the old Roman fort of Othona, now Bradwell-on-Sea. It was a similar story in Northumberland, where the fort of Ebchester was given to St Sampson, and in Wales, where a local prince gave the fort at Holyhead to the Cornish saint and bishop Cybi. And indeed in East Anglia, King Sigeberht also gave the Celtic missionary St Fursey (or Fursa) the old Roman fort at *Cnobheresburg* (widely believed to be Burgh Castle) as a place to build his monastery.

The Walton Castle site also has one other important factor in its favour, namely the fort is on the Colneis peninsular midway between the River Deben and the estuary of the Rivers Orwell and Stour. And the Deben is the river that flowed past Rendlesham, near modern Woodbridge, where the Wuffinga kings had a palace, as well as the nearby Sutton Hoo Saxon cemetery. Sutton Hoo is best known for the ship burial of King Raedwald, the first Wuffinga monarch to be baptised as a Christian, and a man who was also recognised as the Bretwalda (or overlord) of all of England. Given the importance of this area as a seat of Wuffinga regnal power and prestige, it seems all the more likely King Sigeberht would want his new Christian bishop – Felix – to also be based nearby.

Further support for the contention Dommoc was located at Walton, and not Dunwich, comes in the works of the church chronicler the Venerable Bede. He was writing of these events only half a century after they happened and recorded that Felix obtained teachers from the kingdom of Kent to supply the school founded in East Anglia by King Sigeberht. Rochester in Kent was then the closest bishopric to East Anglia by the sea-route from Kent to the Deben.

Finally, in the late eleventh century, as part of his rebuilding project for the old fort at Walton, which he then owned, the Norman baron Roger Bigod invited monks from Kent to establish a priory in the grounds of Walton Castle which was dedicated to St Felix.

Now it is reasonable to assume that if Dommoc was Dunwich, it is highly unlikely a second bishopric would be established at South

Elmham, which is a mere sixteen miles away. However if Dommoc was Walton, then the geography makes more sense as South Elmham is forty miles away.

There is also another theory, which I also find unconvincing, namely that Elmham may have been a twin-centred diocese from the outset – with one seat at South Elmham (forty miles from Walton) and the other at North Elmham, which is in turn forty miles further north from South Elmham, and so neatly and evenly divides up what was then the Kingdom of East Anglia.

A Timeline for the Old Minster

One way or another South Elmham was once the site of a major ecclesiastical establishment, possibly the second East Anglian bishopric of Elmham, until the Viking incursion. Its layout dates back to the style of the seventh century and even its name – the Old Minster – is redolent of former glories.

For example the *Anglo-Saxon Chronicle*, in an entry relating to the Kingdom of Wessex, talks about the consecration of the New Minster in Winchester but this 'New Minster' was actually the West Saxon cathedral. In this context, it would therefore be perfectly logical for the South Elmham Old Minster to be the name given to the building that was formerly the cathedral of Elmham after the see was relocated to the new cathedral at North Elmham.

It therefore becomes possible to assemble a timeline for the Old Minster site, starting with a timber construction in the mid-seventh century but then replaced with a stone building in the early ninth century that replicated the layout of the original building, complete with its archaic design. This building was then reinforced, making it a potential place of refuge and defence when the first Viking raids swept into East Anglia in the 840s.

It has been suggested the unfilled 'putlock holes' (which held the timber scaffolding used during a church's construction – once the building was complete, they would be filled in and plastered over) in some of the walls at the Old Minster indicate the ninth century building was still unfinished when the Viking incursion destroyed the diocese. And then the Old Minster remained a ruin until the late eleventh century when Herbert de Losinga came onto the scene, acquiring the manor of South Elmham and establishing an episcopal chapel there, close by the location of his summer retreat and Bishop's Palace at South Elmham Hall.

So does this explanation solve the mystery of the Old Minster? That the long-derelict ecclesiastical ruins at South Elmham were once the cathedral serving the Elmham diocese from its earliest days until the catastrophe of the Viking invasion some two hundred years later. There's also a certain congruity here if Herbert de Losinga had private episcopal chapels built on the sites of both the old cathedral at North Elmham *and* the even earlier cathedral at South Elmham. Were these chapels to celebrate the sacred memory of the distinctly troubled Christian tradition in East Anglia?

But this does not explain why this relatively obscure, isolated hilltop on the southern edge of the Waveney valley was selected in the first place as the location for the Old Minster.

What was the attraction of this particular site? Had there been something there before? And had this something anything to do with the fact that, during pagan Saxon times, the land surrounding what would later become the Old Minster was used for burials? Or that before even the Saxons arrived, there was a Roman fort on this site? We'll be looking at these issues in the next chapter.

CHAPTER 13

A HILLTOP IN SUFFOLK

Of all the remote hilltops along the perimeter of the Waveney valley in the latter part of the seventh century, why did Bishop Bedwinus, the first bishop of the new diocese of Elmham, select the Old Minster site at South Elmham?

Was it because there was already something there to make it special or sacred? Similarly, why did the pagan Saxons pick this site for a cemetery? What made it special? And, winding back the historical clock by another four centuries, why did the Roman legions choose to build a fort on this site, during their reoccupation of East Anglia in the aftermath of Boudicca's revolt?

Clearly it would have been a deliberate decision by the Romans but it doesn't appear to make any strategic sense. The Romans definitely were in this part of East Anglia. For example, they founded the nearby town of Bungay, which occupies strategically valuable high ground overlooking a bend on the River Waveney. There was also an important Roman road running through this part of England: the old Pye Road which ran south from *Venta Icenorum* (just south of modern-day Norwich) via *Villa Faustini* (near the village of Scole), the fort at *Combretovium* (near Balyham House in Suffolk, a few miles from Ipswich), then on to *Camulodunum* (Colchester), *Caesaromagus* (Chelmsford), and finally into *Londinium* (London). This is basically the same route the modern A140 and A12 roads take.

Bungay lies just five miles to the east of the Old Minster site, while *Villa Faustini*/Scole is eleven miles to the west, but neither of them offers any strategic rationale for a fort at South Elmham. There therefore has to be another reason why the Romans felt it was necessary to construct a fort in that location.

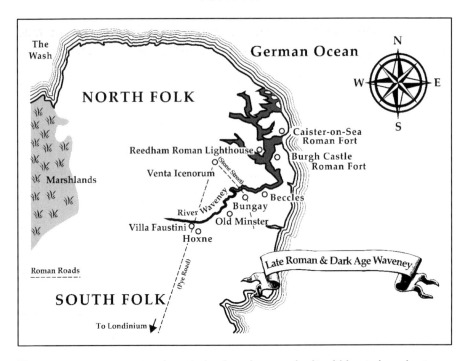

If it was not strategic, then it had to be symbolic. Was it by placing a fort there, the all-conquering Roman Empire was making a point to the local Celtic Iceni tribe – Boudicca's people – that they'd just been defeated by a more powerful and superior civilisation who could do anything they wanted, including building a fort on top of a sacred Celtic site?

We know from the archaeological evidence the nearby Flixton gravel terraces were a centre of ritual ceremony and reverence for the dead from 2,500 BC in the Bronze Age. We also know Neolithic, Bronze Age and Iron Age finds, including a bronze axe-head and an Iceni coin, have been discovered in the South Elmham area. Neolithic communities also favoured hilltop sites. And we know that to-date no archaeological evidence has been found to suggest the Old Minster site was once an Iceni civic or military centre.

That leaves just one alternative: it was a ritual or sacred site. A holy site the Romans desecrated, just as they defiled Boudicca's daughters, to teach the rebellious barbarian tribesmen a lesson they would not forget in a hurry. And when the Roman army established its camp on what would later become the Old Minster site at South Elmham, that camp would have, from the outset, featured a shrine or altar.

With the departure of the Roman legions and the collapse of Romano-British society in the face of the Saxon incursions, the situation at the Old Minster site changed again.

The early Saxons worshipped in places where they felt the landscape had a liminal aspect that brought them closer to the supernatural. These places included hilltops, springs and wells, and woodland groves and clearings. They even reused existing hallowed sites, such as abandoned temples, standing stones, and Neolithic and Bronze Age burial mounds and barrows.

The Saxons also had something they called the *hearg* (or *heargh*) which was a sacred sanctuary or tribal cult site. Harrow on the Hill, now in North-West London and home to the famous Harrow public school, derives its name from having once been the hilltop site of a pagan Saxon *hearg*. *Heargs* were the equivalent of the later Christian churchyard or 'God's Acre' although for the Saxons, who did also use them as burial grounds for a select number of high-status individuals, these sites could be extensive.

Now let's revisit the Old Minster site at South Elmhall. It is on top of a hill. It was already a sacred site for the Celts. It is set within the boundaries of an old Roman fort, creating an ideal delineation for a *hearg*.

It was the site of a number, but not a large number, of early Saxon burials or at least the interment of pottery urns 'filled with burnt bones and ashes [which] seems to confirm the voice of tradition very current in the village, that the Minster occupies the site of a pagan temple,' to quote the antiquarian, the Reverend Alfred Suckling (another member of Lord Nelson's mother's family) in his book *The History and Antiquities of The County of Suffolk*.

There is also some evidence to suggest that on the edges of the River Waveney, at nearby Flixton, there may have a hall belonging the local ruling Saxon dynasty, the Wuffingas.

And the place name South Elmham is derived from the Anglo-Saxon for 'the place (hamlet, estate or manor) where the elms grow'. Even today, part of the magic and mystery of the Old Minster ruins is that they are in a clearing within a grove of trees.

As to who or what the Saxons worshipped at South Elmham, the most likely candidate is Woden. Not only was Woden a widely-worshipped Saxon god but he was also claimed to be an ancestor of the local Wuffinga ruling dynasty. Saxon genealogies name a certain Wehha, the leader of a band of migrants from Frisia, as the first ruler of East Anglia in the sixth century. Although Wehha is best known as the father of King Wuffa (who was ruling by 571) who gave his name to the Wuffinga dynasty, according to Wehha's own family tree, he was the great-great-great-great-great grandson of the god Woden.

Wehha, incidentally, also has another claim to fame, namely that he has been identified with Weohstan (or Wihstan), the father of Wiglaf, one of the heroes of the Anglo-Saxon epic poem *Beowulf*. As for Woden, although his worship may have been driven out by St Felix and the other Christian missionaries of the seventh century, his legacy lives on, and not just as the god who gave his name to Wednesday. The white-bearded Woden, who rode the midwinter sky on his eight-footed steed Sleipnir, visiting his people with gifts, is believed to be one of the origins of the Santa Claus/Father Christmas tradition.

All of which brings us back to where we started this chapter, namely asking why did Bishop Bedwinus, the first bishop of the new diocese of Elmham, select the Old Minster site at South Elmham? With so much pagan legacy from the Saxons and the Romans, you might have thought this would have been a place to avoid and that the Church would have wanted to establish itself on virgin land untainted by the worship of other gods?

The answer can be found in a letter Pope Gregory gave to Abbot Mellitus (later the first Bishop of London and, later still, an Archbishop of Canterbury) in 601 when he was about to join Augustine's mission in England. In the letter, Pope Gregory gives instructions on how to convert the Anglo-Saxons, suggesting a pragmatic, if not a little cynical, shift from a policy of compulsory conversion to the more subtle one of cultural and psychological persuasion or 'acculturation'. The letter reads:

> Tell Augustine that he should by no means destroy the temples of the gods but rather the idols within those temples. Let him, after he has purified them with holy water, place altars and relics of the saints in them. For, if those temples are well built, they should be converted from the worship of demons to the service of the true God. Thus, seeing that their places of worship are not destroyed, the people will banish error from their hearts and come to places familiar and dear to them in acknowledgement and worship of the true God.

> Further, since it has been their custom to slaughter oxen in sacrifice, they should receive some solemnity in exchange. Let them therefore, on the day of the dedication of their churches, or on the feast of the martyrs whose relics are preserved in them, build themselves huts around their one-time temples and celebrate the occasion with religious feasting. They will sacrifice and eat the animals not any more as an offering to the devil, but for the glory of God to whom, as the giver of all things, they will give thanks for having been satiated. Thus, if they are not deprived of all exterior joys, they will more easily taste the interior ones. For surely it is impossible to efface all at once everything from their strong minds, just as, when one wishes to reach the top of a mountain, he must climb by stages and step by step, not by leaps and bounds...

In other words, instead of destroying temples and outlawing animal sacrifices, which had certainly been the policy of many early Christian missionaries, Gregory was now advocating converting pagan temples and sacred groves into Christian churches and places of worship, as well as changing sacrifices into Christian feast days.

Given this scenario, rather than avoiding what we now call the Old Minster site at South Elmham (there is no indication of any previous Christian activity at the site during the later Roman period) it was by Pope Gregory's recommendations the perfect location to establish a new church, as it could build upon its already established legacy as a sacred site. A case of telling the locals 'You know you used to climb up that hill to worship at a pagan shrine? Well you can still pray on that hill only now it will be before a Christian altar.'

The Sun also Rises

Now it is time to go back one step further in history to explore the reasons why South Elmham may have been an important sacred site to the Celtic Iceni tribe before the Romans arrived in the Waveney valley.

Of all the deities worshipped by the pre-Roman Britons – the Celts – one of the most widely venerated was the sun god, or god of light, Belenus. (Or Bel – other spelling variants include Belenos, Belinus, Beil, and the Welsh Beli Mawr.) There have been more archaeological finds associated with Belenus in Continental Europe, Britain, and Ireland than any other Celtic god, suggesting he was the common god in Celtic culture until the advent of Christianity.

The name of the pre-Roman king Cunobelinus is derived from 'hound of Belenus'. Cunobelinus, or Cunobeline, was the basis for Shakespeare's play *Cymbeline* – his son was the even more famous King Caractactus who led the military opposition to the Roman invasion of Britain in AD 43. Meanwhile the notoriously fanciful medieval historian Geoffrey of Monmouth refers to a legendary and, almost certainly, totally fictional Dark Age king of England called Belinus the Great in his twelfth century book *The History of the Kings of Britain*.

Ironically it is primarily the Romans, and Julius Caesar in particular, we have to thank for what knowledge we do have of the Celtic gods. This is because the Celtic tribal society of pre-Roman England was a pre-literate world where an oral rather than written culture prevailed. Thanks to their dealings with the Gallic Celts on the other side of the English Channel in Gaul (what is now France and Belgium) there was some use of writing within the English Celtic kingdoms, such as the use of Latin inscriptions on coins.

It would appear the priesthood – the Druids – had an entirely oral culture. In Caesar's *Commentaries on the Gallic War* (*Comentarii de Bello Gallico* – his multi-volume account of the nine years he spent fighting in Gaul) several chapters are devoted to the Druids and their superstitions. It was Caesar who first recorded the details of the Celts offering human sacrifices and burning their victims in giant wicker men.

According to Caesar, Druidic lore consisted of many verses learned by heart and it could take novices up to twenty years to complete their studies. He also suggests the Druids' beliefs forbad them from recording their knowledge in written form. The net result is not one certifiably ancient verse of Druidic lore is known to have survived, even in translation. What we are left with is archaeological evidence, such as inscriptions on temple ruins, tombs and springs across Europe, from the north of England to Spain, and across Gaul and into northern Italy, commemorating Belenus as 'the Fair Shining One' and 'the Shining God'.

The absence of any contemporary Celtic chronicles of Druidic belief systems means we have to rely on secondhand sources, such the Romans and even later Christian missionaries. But these are often little more than myths and unreliable hearsay or else, as in the case of the missionaries, devoid of their original religious meaning, with Celtic gods downgraded to demons.

MAY DAY

The Victorian-era depiction of robed Druids worshipping at altars in front of giant standing stones is just another example of romantic wishful thinking. Sites like Stonehenge were actually constructed some 2,000 to 2,500 years before the Druids and Celts even arrived on the British historical scene. While the Celts may have reused earlier sacred sites for their own rituals, the fact there are no – and never have been – any monoliths at South Elmham does not preclude it from being a Celtic religious site.

The traditional view is the Celts practised their religion in natural settings, in the open air, erecting shrines in remote areas such as beside lakes, on hilltops, and within groves of trees – the latter two being characteristics of the South Elmham site. But there is another aspect of the worship of the god Belenus, which plays a key role in unravelling of the mystery of the Old Minister site and that is the festival of Beltane on May 1st.

The names Belenus and Beltane clearly have a common etymological root although since the early twentieth century the accepted theory has been that the 'bel' element is derived from a common Celtic (and subsequently Old Irish and Old English) word *bhel* or *belo*, meaning bright fire, shining or white. This makes sense as Belenus was a fair, bright and shining solar god and Beltane was originally a fire festival. By way of a further connection, the seventeenth century Irish historian Geoffrey Keating said that in medieval times Beltane was the occasion to make sacrifices to a god named Beil, while another explanation is that the word Beltane is derived from the phrase 'the fires of Bel'.

Since the late twentieth century, Beltane has enjoyed a revival thanks to the activities of Wiccans, Neopagans, Celtic Reconstructionists, and Neo-Druids who all regard it as one of the key sabbats or seasonal festivals of the Wheel of the Year. The fact it is now also an important cultural/social event in some parts of the United Kingdom (such as the annual Beltane Fire Festival that has been running in Edinburgh for thirty years) has also helped revived its popularity.

That said, there are enough accounts of Beltane both from ancient sources, such as the tenth century Irish manuscript *Sanas Cormaic,* and from writers, antiquarians and folklorists collecting stories from the eighteenth and on into the early twentieth century to piece together the main elements of traditional Beltane customs.

The May 1st date is significant as in the Northern Hemisphere it lies midway between the Spring (or Vernal) Equinox, usually around March 21st, and Summer Solstice (or longest day) on or around June 21st. Beltane was traditionally the start of the summer and the time when pastoral herdsmen (as the Celts were) would drive their cattle out to graze in their summer pastures.

Among the rituals – particularly strong in Ireland, the Isle of Man and the Scottish Highlands – associated with Beltane was the lighting of two large bonfires, between which a farmer's cattle would then be driven. Other variations included building just one large bonfire and driving the cattle around it – or even making the cattle jump through the flames. And not just cattle, as people would also dance around (in a strictly clockwise, sunwise or *deiseil* direction) and jump over bonfires, as their flames, smoke and ashes were believed to have protective powers.

According to Sir James George Frazer in his 1890 classic *The Golden Bough: A Study in Magic and Religion*, the fire rituals were a kind of imitative or sympathetic magic to mimic the Sun (we're back to Belenus the solar deity again) and ensure a plentiful supply of sunshine. This was thought to ensure healthy and abundant livestock and crops over the coming summer months, and/or to symbolically burn and destroy all harmful influences, including disease and the malicious influence of evil fairies and witches, so both animals and people were purified, protected and more potent.

There was undoubtedly also a fertility ritual aspect to the Beltane, a kind of Celtic *Relight My Fire*. For example there was a widespread belief the British Isles that if a young woman washed her face in the dew on the grass on Beltane morning, it would increase her sexual attractiveness.

This picture is muddied by the overlap between Beltane and the more sexually blatant celebrations of May Day. These included dancing around distinctly phallic maypoles, crowning the May Queen, and Jack-in-the-Green, all of which may stem from Saxon tree worship. There was also 'maying' when young men and women would go into the woods on May Eve to gather flowers to be made into garlands for May Day decorations – although by the sixteenth century maying had become an euphemism for bawdy outdoor sexual activity. Maying probably has origins dating back to the ancient

Roman festival of Floralia (April 28ᵗʰ to May 3ʳᵈ) a licentious fertility festival, involving plenty of alcohol and nudity but at least the participants wore flowers in their hair.

Did the Beltane fires also harken back to more primitive times when human sacrifice was still practised? This theory does depend on the veracity of Caesar's accounts of Druids and their wicker men. That said Beltane is reputed to be a liminal time of the year when the boundaries between this world of the living and the 'Otherworld' of the dead and the supernatural become more porous.

But now let's return to another aspect of the story: the St Michael and St Mary Alignment and the two saints associated with this ley-line.

Chapter 14

Into the Heart of the Sunrise

There is a long tradition in Europe that Christian churches are built – or orientated – on an east-west axis, give or take a few degrees either way to account for the inevitable inaccuracy of the measurement. The word 'orientation' is from Latin *oriens,* from *orientum* meaning 'the rising sun'.

As the Archbishop of Milan, Charles Borromeo, explained in the mid-sixteenth century, the 'Easting' process also required churches to be orientated in line with the rising sun on either the Spring or Autumnal equinoxes and not at the solstices.

Based on this east-west layout, the chancel and the altar are always located at the eastern end, while the nave is at the western end – an arrangement which means the congregation are facing east when they pray. Why? There are at least three traditions to explain the orientation of churches and why the altar is at the east.

The first is the church is facing the celestial city of Jerusalem, which for most people in the Roman Empire and, later Roman Catholic Church, would have been in the east.

The second explanation is Christ's second coming would be on the clouds coming from the east: 'For as the lightning cometh out of the east, and shineth even unto the west; so shall also the coming of the Son of man be.' (Matthew 24:27.) Burials in Christian churches and churchyards are still normally aligned so the deceased's feet face east, the intention being that on the Day of Resurrection, the dead would be able to rise up facing their Maker.

There is also a third explanation saying the significance of the east stems from the belief mankind's original home, the Garden of Eden, lay in the east.

As to the accuracy of the east-west orientation, the most recent study I've read, reported in *The Antiquaries Journal* magazine in 2001, found that out of a survey of 1,750 churches in England and Wales the average deviation from due East was just four degrees. This is remarkably good as the earlier builders would have been relying on sighting sticks, while the first compasses, which were of questionable quality, did not appear in Western Europe until around the year 1300.

Inevitably there were some exceptions. Churches built within towns and cities were constrained by the location of neighbouring buildings, while those in rural areas had to accommodate the natural topography. For example in marshy areas, such as the Fens of eastern England, churches would be built on higher, firmer ground. Similarly, churches built in valleys would be oriented to take advantage of the best natural light source on a morning, regardless of from which direction it came.

There was also one very important deliberate exception, namely those churches that were orientated towards the point on the horizon where the sun rose on the feast day of the saint to whom the church was dedicated. So, for example, a church dedicated to St Edmund the Martyr, the unfortunate king of East Anglia who was killed by the Vikings, would be aligned in the direction the sun rose on November 20th, which is his official feast day.

Incidentally, before you go rushing off to measure the orientation of your local church, it is worth noting many of these churches now appear to give wildly inaccurate readings.

This is typically because the original orientation was calculated under the older Julian (or Old Style/OS) calendar, which was the prevailing standard in England until 1752, whereas the newer Gregorian (or New Style/NS) calendar is thirteen days ahead of Julian. So, for example, to verify if a pre-1752 church dedicated to St Edmund was really aligned with sunrise on his feast day (November 20th Old Style), you would have to take your reading almost a fortnight later on December 3rd New Style.

There is also another reason for a discrepancy on feast day orientations and that is down to the surprising number of churches that have changed their dedications over the centuries, either by accident or design, so the current patron saint is not the one the church was originally dedicated to when it was built.

For example, a few miles to the west of the town of Diss, not far from the source of the River Waveney, are the villages of North Lopham and South Lopham. In North Lopham stands the church of St Nicholas, while one mile away in South Lopham stands the church of St Andrew, complete with the largest Norman church tower (it look more like a castle keep) in Norfolk. When these churches were first built, South Lopham was dedicated to St Nicholas and St Andrew was the North Lopham church. In fact, you can still see a crowned letter 'A' for Andrew on the North Lopham church tower.

The explanation for this strange swapping of dedications is during the eighteenth century, when church dedications were coming back into fashion after the English Reformation and later Puritan austerity of the mid-seventeenth century, a couple of parsons, dabbling in antiquarian research into the history of the buildings, mistakenly transposed the dedications.

ASTRONOMY DOMINE

Unfortunately (and I say unfortunately because getting to grasp with the maths coming up makes my brain hurt) there is also another more complex and cosmic reason why sunrises do not coincide with the feast days of patron saints, even when the dedications of churches have not been changed but the difference between the Julian and Gregorian calendars have been factored in.

To understand the reason we need to look to the stars, literally, and delve into some astronomy. Not my favourite topic, as I was a duffer at geometry when I was at school, and my ignorance is highlighted by the fact we are now going to visit at a concept first expounded by a Greek astronomer called Hipparchus, who lived on the island of

Rhodes sometime around the year 150 BC. There are suggestions the Chaldeans and the ancient Egyptians may have made similar discoveries even earlier in mankind's history.

The planet Earth rotates on its axis approximately once every 24 hours, in other words once a day, and revolves around the Sun once every year – or approximately every 365 days. But only approximately: the annual orbit around the Sun actually takes 365.24 days, which is why we have a leap year every four years to deal with that extra quarter of a day. It is also why we had the Gregorian calendar replacing the earlier Julian version, which dealt with the extra quarter of a day a little less accurately.

Not only does the Earth spin on its axis but it spins at an angle – known as its axial tilt – currently 23.44 degrees in respect to its orbital plain. (Or the 'obliquity of the ecliptic' to use the technical term.) Forget the technical terminology, it is the consequences that are important because it is this tilt that gives Earth is four seasons – and also explains why when it is winter in the Northern Hemisphere, it is summer in the Southern Hemisphere.

There is also a further complication in that not only does the Earth tilt but the axial tilt also varies between 22.1 degrees and 24.5 degrees over a cycle lasting about 41,000 years. This axial precession (meaning the change in the orientation of the rotational axis of a spinning body) is caused by the gravitational pull of the Sun and the Moon. And, it should be noted, the Earth's annual orbit around the Sun is also mildly elliptical.

To sum up, the net result is instead of the Earth neatly spinning consistently and vertically, like a top, it leans over, wobbling and pitching on its axis.

For practical purposes none of this matters a jot to us because the changes are so imperceptible as to have no impact upon our daily lives. On a longer-term basis however it means the location of sunrise at an ancient site or church's orientation changes by about one degree every 72 years, which is the equivalent to a change of one day every hundred years. So, for example, if you were to compare the sunrise in 2020 at a church that had been aligned with sunrise on its patron saint's feast day when it was built in 1300, there would be a ten-degree or seven day discrepancy.

But, returning now to the Old Minster, what is the orientation of this building? It is clearly not the East as it is aligned at 59.75 degrees, which is a massive 30.25 degrees out of alignment with true East, a margin of error too great to have been an accident. But if it was deliberate, what was the purpose behind it?

According to Suffolk-based retired medic-turned-local historian Dr Basil Harrold, who in 2002 made a field trip at dawn to South Elmham, in the year 900 the sun would have risen in line with the orientation of the Old Minster in early May.

As there are so many variables involved, it is almost impossible to predict the exact date – not least because with the Old Minster we don't know exactly when it was built. Nevertheless, an orientation date of early May does throw out an intriguing possibility because on May 1st (May Day or Beltane) the rising sun is in direct alignment with the route of the St Michael ley-line. It's also worth noting the Old Minster's skewed 30.25 degrees orientation is very close to that of the St Michael line, which averages a very similar 28 degrees north-of-east orientation across its 350 mile length.

The Old Minster's orientation is so far out of alignment with true east that it must be deliberate rather than as a result of an error. But, similarly, the fact it both shares almost the same orientation of the St Michael ley and is orientated towards sunrise in early May is also far too much of a coincidence to be an accident.

So is its orientation the key to the mystery of the Old Minster? That it was aligned to the rising sun shining down the St Michael ley-line (or at least the more tangible eastern extension of the Icknield Way) at the beginning of May? At Beltane, the start of the summer, the midpoint between the Spring Equinox and Summer Solstice? The time when Neolithic and later Celtic herdsmen would drive out their cattle to graze on their summer pastures, which in this part of the world would have been the water meadows of the Waveney valley.

The time when Bronze Age travellers and merchants heading out from the East of England would have the longest days still ahead of them for making their way to and back from the West Country and the tin mines of Cornwall.

And the time, during the even earlier Neolithic era, when nomadic hunter-gatherers would begin their annual westerly migration across the Doggerland land-bridge between Continental Europe and the British Isles, entering the country via what is now the Norfolk-Suffolk coast, with the Waveney valley opening up before them as a gateway to their summer hunting grounds.

As for the Old Minster site itself? Topographically, it would have occupied a compact, secluded site with easy access to fresh water from a nearby stream, about twenty miles – or a day's trek – from the coast.

For bands of nomads entering from Doggerland, it would have therefore made an ideal location for an overnight camp at the end of their first day. And as the sun came up on their second day, a place to give thanks to their gods and goddesses (solar and lunar deities whose identity we cannot even pretend to guess) for their safe deliverance from the terrors of the night, such as bears, wolves and sabre-tooth cats.

To the people of those times, this would have seemed like a magical, mysterious, if not downright miraculous phenomenon – and it also explains why there were pagan shrines and cemeteries in the area in the pre-Roman Celtic era, as well as the later punitive Roman camp and the subsequent Saxon and Christian occupations of the South Elmham site.

It may be just be a hilltop in Suffolk but it is a hilltop that embodies over 7,000 years of tradition and ritual, dating back to the days of the long-last Doggerland land-bridge when sunrise at the beginning of May illuminated a safe route across England to the southwest. No wonder the first post-Roman Christians built the Old Minster there.

EPILOGUE

FOOTPRINTS IN THE SANDS OF TIME

Our journey began in an unprepossessing ditch several miles to the west of the market town of Diss but ended on a beach on the coast of East Anglia, looking out across the North Sea.

It is an appropriate place to end our journey, standing at the most easterly part of the United Kingdom – nowadays called the Sunrise Coast – watching the sun come up over the horizon on May Day to illuminate not just the Waveney valley, the enigmatic ruins of the Old Minster, and the haunts of Black Shuck, but also the path of the St Michael and St Mary ley-line all the way across England to Cornwall and its once treasured tin mines.

It is also an appropriate place to end this book because it is also here, on this East Anglian beach, that whole story of the British Isles began. It was here that after the Ice Ages had ended, the repopulation of the land began, with our Neolithic hunter-gatherer ancestors returning across the now long-lost Doggerland land-bridge from Continental Europe.

It was also here, at what is now the beach at Happisburgh on the Norfolk Coast, that 800,000 years ago some unknown hominins, members of an archaic and long-vanished human species, left their footprints in the sands of time, where they remained hidden until 2013.

And, bringing this more up-to-date, it brings up the hairs on the back of your neck to realise that just eighty years ago, the Bloody Hundredth and other aircraft of the USAAF would have been following the path of the St Michael and St Mary Alignment – into the sunrise on their way out, into the sunset on their return, from their bombing raids over Continental Europe. Perhaps that's why Eddie the Ghost is still at Thorpe Abbotts?

Appendix 1:

All You Ever Wanted to Know About Ley-Lines But Were Afraid to Ask

For the purposes of this book, I'm completely open-minded and non-judgmental about the concept of ley-lines so let's start with a basic definition: A ley-line is the supposed alignment of many places of geographical and historical interest (such as ancient monuments, outcrops of rock and crest of hills) that since ancient times have marked trackways used for trade, ceremonial or mystical purposes.

The Old Straight Track

The first proponent of ley-lines in this country was the amateur archaeologist and photographer Alfred Watkins who, in 1921, published a book called *The Old Straight Track*. Based on his landscape observations, map reading and measurements of the English countryside, he put forward the theory that many places of geographical and historical interest were aligned in a straight line and that these lines formed the routes of ancient trackways.

Watkins explained that one day, while looking at a Roman camp site and studying a map, he saw 'like a chain of fairy lights' a series of straight alignments of various ancient features (such as standing stones, wayside crosses, causeways, hill forts, castles, ancient churches on mounds, barrows, cairns, stone circles, moats, springs, fords, wells) and realised many footpaths also seemed to connect one hilltop to another in a straight line.

From here was born the concept of the ley line as a form of ancient navigation aid. Watkins believed that, in prehistoric times when England was far more densely forested, the country was criss-crossed by a network of straight line tracks, with prominent natural

and man-made landscape features being used as navigation points by travellers.

Some English ley-lines also coincide with old funeral or coffin paths, otherwise known as spirit ways and corpse roads, which would be followed by mourners carrying a coffin to a graveyard for burial. A good English example is the Lyke Wake Walk across the North Yorkshire Moors, which this author singularly failed to complete in 1967.

161

More recently M.J. Harper and H.L. Vered in their book *The Megalithic Empire* suggested that ley-lines and the many stone circles or henges (and the even more common but now largely lost wood circles) once formed a cohesive nationwide navigation system, with individual stones in a henge being the Neolithic and Bronze Age equivalent of direction signposts on a modern highway roundabout.

Watkins himself never attributed any supernatural significance to leys, he merely believed they were pathways used for trade or ceremonial purposes since ancient times. But the ley-hunters who follows Watkins began to blend a more mystic element into the mix.

THE FENG SHUI OF THE LANDSCAPE

By the 1960s many ley-hunters had become involved in a 'Which-came-first-the-chicken-or-the-egg?' debate over whether the lines were created by the alignment of landscape features and monuments or whether the monuments and features followed pre-existing magnetic lines and Earth energy fields.

The late John Michell pulled all these esoteric ideas together in his 1969 book *The View Over Atlantis*, describing them as part of a system of geomantic beliefs and Earth mysteries related to Chinese dragon paths (or dragon lines) and Feng Shui. Michell's use of the term 'dragon lines' is also intriguing because St Michael is a 'dragon saint' (in common with St George) frequently depicted slaying a dragon in religious iconography. (There are actually over forty saints in the Western Christian tradition who supposedly either killed or expelled dragons according to accounts of their lives.)

This more esoteric theory, with its key global nodal points of Stonehenge in England, Uluru/Ayers Rock in Australia, the Nazca lines in Peru, and the Great Pyramid in Egypt, rapidly became more popular than the Watkins explanation and was soon wrapped up with other New Age (cynics would call it 'woo-woo') occult beliefs and mysticism, including UFO sightings. Michell's book is also credited with putting Glastonbury and its Tor on the counterculture map both literally and metaphorically.

BAD SCIENCE

There is a third explanation for ley-lines and that is they can all be explained away in terms of chance alignments, coincidences, and just plain bad science. For example, there is no independent, objective, scientific evidence to support the contention that ley-lines are the source of power, energy or even natural magnetic fields.

More damning still is the fact that many ley-lines are really not straight lines anyway. The issue here is maps are a two-dimensional representation of a three-dimensional landscape so, depending upon the scale of the map, an element of distortion exists with the result that while three points may appear to be aligned, in reality they are not. It has even been suggested that the pencils Watkins used to trace his original ley-lines had such thick leads that they alone created a fifty feet margin of error.

Add all these criticisms together and you find that many supposed ley-lines on a map actually encompass an area several hundreds of yards wide, so it is hardly-surprising they frequently clip multiple historic sites. To go back to Watkins' pencils, a ley-line is more like a wide-tipped whiteboard marker than a 2H pencil line.

A further problem for fans of ley-lines is in England, because there are so many archaeological sites, you can draw a line virtually anywhere on a map and it will run through several. There is nothing magical about this, it is just a matter of chance alignment.

There is no esoteric mystery surrounding the siting of telephone boxes yet, if you track them on a map, you will find many of them appear to be aligned. It has also been observed that postcodes coincide with ley-lines, the location of former Woolworths stores in the West Midlands seem to create strange geometrical patterns, while in the United States there is an internet meme showing that by carefully plotting branches of the Outback Steakhouse chain you can create a series of giant pentagrams across the map on North America.

Possibly the biggest credibility problem for ley-lines is why they contain marker points (monuments etc) of such widely differing historical dates. For example the 350-mile long St Michael Ley which runs across England in a northeasterly direction from Lands End, a natural phenomenon, via St Michael's Mount, another natural feature but with mediaeval additions, the Bronze Age Hurlers stone circle, Glastonbury Tor, an Iron Age hill fort, the Avebury Henge, Woolpit (the location for William of Newburgh's story of the two green children) and mediaeval Bury St Edmunds Cathedral before running into the North Sea at Hopton-on-Sea on the Norfolk Coast.

LEY-LINES AND UFOS

Fans of the esoteric/Earth mysteries explanation of ley-lines will also tell you that it is possible to feel the energy surging along their length and that if you stand at a primary node it positively crackles. I've stood on plenty of ley-lines – and even leaned up against the ancient monoliths – but have never felt anything. Perhaps tuning in to the energy fields requires the honing of those psi/PK psychic/psychokinetic powers we are all said to possess, such as the ability of dowsers to locate underground water?

Whatever the explanation, ley-lines are said to be a focal point for both paranormal phenomenon and UFO (unidentified flying objects, such as alien spacecraft) activity, the latter apparently following the route of the energy fields. So what is the situation regarding UFOs over the Waveney valley?

While there has never been a shortage of sightings of lights in the sky over the Waveney valley most of these have mundane, terrestrial explanations. These range from international civilian air traffic flying in and out of Amsterdam Schipol Airport in the Netherlands, which lies almost directly east of the Waveney valley; through to military aircraft flying off the North Sea and along the Waveney valley either en route for the American bases at Mildenhall and Lakenheath or else for training exercises over the STANTA Stanford Battle Area near Thetford. There was even one occasion when the coloured 'skytracker' searchlights above a night-club, reflecting off low cloud, prompted a UFO scare.

But, we do have the Rendlesham Forest Incident, which occurred in late December 1980. Although the forest is about twenty-five miles south of the Waveney Valley, it has to be mentioned as, to date, it is the UK's most famous alleged UFO incident – and in fact is widely referred to as 'Britain's Roswell'.

Sadly over forty years later we are still none-the-wiser as to what actually happened. Was it an actual UFO landing? Was it merely the lights of the nearby Orford Ness lighthouse flashing through the forest? Was it a fireball, possibly a meteoroid burning up in the sky – one was seen over southern England at around the time of the first Rendlesham 'UFO sighting'. Was it the lights of the nearby RAF Bentwaters airbase? Was it a hoax? Or was it even a misunderstanding prompted by US Air Force staff at nearby RAF Woodbridge (both the Bentwaters and Woodbridge bases were on the edge of the forest) blundering into a military exercise (possibly conducted by the SAS) involving lasers and holograms?

In the forty years that have elapsed, eye-witness accounts have changed, usually for the more dramatic – and indeed some supposed eye-witnesses have proved to have been nowhere near the forest or the bases when the incident occurred. Meanwhile a cottage industry has grown up in terms of books (and more recently TV shows and movies) about the event, all helped by the fact the official response of the Ministry of Defence was opaque in content, creating the impression of a cover-up even where there may have been nothing to cover-up.

The Bentwaters based has now closed and the US Air Force has now left Woodbridge (although it is still used by the British Army so is closed to the public) and even the Orford Ness lighthouse has been demolished. However Forestry England has now created a 'UFO Trail' through Rendlesham Forest, complete with a fake UFO in a picnic site.

Appendix 2:

Meet the Bigod Family - and their Castles

We first encountered the Bigods at the beginning of this book, where we saw Roger Bigod trick his way into seizing St Benet's Abbey but what happened next? And how did the Bigod family fare over the following years and centuries?

Despite the fact we are dealing with a family who lived and died nearly a thousand years ago, in many respects they were a thoroughly modern family of ruthless back-stabbers, liars and rogues who always had an eye on the main chance and didn't care who they had to trample over or betray to achieve it. In an era of ever-so fickle monarchs, when a favourite could fall from power overnight and the following morning find their head skewered at the end of a spear, staring sightlessly into the rising sun, the Bigods were masters of surviving a real-life mediaeval *Game of Thrones* – and of keeping their heads while those all around were losing theirs.

Roger Bigod (*circa* 1040-1107)

Following his activities at St Benet's, we next run into Roger Bigod two years later, in 1069, when he and two other Norman warlords, including Ralph de Gael (or de Guader), the then Earl of Norfolk and Suffolk, led an army that defeated the Viking king of Denmark Sweyn II Estridsson near Ipswich. For these services, Roger was generously rewarded by King William but this was nothing compared to five years later when Ralph de Gael fell from power in the failed Revolt of the Earls against William and Roger acquired many of the dispossessed de Gael's estates and manors.

The Bigods' obsession: Bungay Castle, it fell into ruin within fifty years of financially ruining the dynasty. Photo: Charles Christian.

In the years that followed, in his capacity as the Sheriff of Norfolk and Suffolk, Roger acquired so much more property that, by the time the *Domesday Book* was completed in 1086, only the king owned more land in East Anglia.

The following year, 1087, William the Conqueror was on his deathbed but, before he died, he ordered his kingdom be split between his eldest son Robert, who became the Duke of Normandy, and his second eldest son William (better known as William Rufus) who took the throne of England as King William II.

As Duke Robert and William Rufus were known to loathe each other (along with the usual sibling rivalry, young Rufus was also guilty of playing practical jokes on Robert, frequently involving the contents of chamber-pots) this presented a problem of divided loyalties for those barons who held estates in both Normandy and England, so a plot was hatched to depose William Rufus and unite the two countries under Duke Robert.

Known as the Rebellion of 1088, it lasted less than six months and saw the rebels, including Roger Bigod of Norfolk, defeated and outmanoeuvred by William thanks to a winning combination (still favoured by politicians today) of good luck, promises and bribery. Unlike the brutal punishment normally inflicted on defeated rebels, William Rufus heeded the advice of the barons who had remained loyal to him and opted for leniency.

In the words of one adviser: 'If you temper your animosity against these great men and treat them graciously here, or permit them to depart in safety, you may advantageously use their amity and service on many future occasions. He who is your enemy now, may be your useful friend another time.'

William Rufus was actually a far smarter king than history credits him as being. Unfortunately history is written by the survivors and, after his premature death, Rufus received a very bad press from the Church, who were practically the only people who could read or write in those days. For Roger Bigod, the aftermath of the rebellion was that although he lost some of his lands, he kept his head and went on to regain those estates when he reconciled with the king.

Roger Bigod outlived William Rufus, who was killed in a never adequately explained hunting accident August 1100 in the New Forest, when he was struck by an arrow (see the next 'Quite Intriguing Too'). We next hear of Roger Bigod being one of the witnesses recorded on the Charter of Liberties which the new monarch Henry I made as part of his coronation promises. The Charter of Liberties is one of those overlooked events in English mediaeval history that can now be seen as a forerunner of the more famous Magna Carta.

That said this was no Bill of Rights for the benefit of the Common Man but rather a series of promises and implicit bribes to mollify the kingdom's earls and barons, who were less than enthusiastic about Henry's accession. Henry was the younger brother of the late William Rufus but many nobles still favoured handing the crown to Duke Robert of Normandy.

Whatever the merits of the coronation charter, it is notable that Roger Bigod remained loyal to the new king when a further unsuccessful attempt was made in 1101 to place Duke Robert on the English throne.

There again, Roger may have been influenced by the fact that following his coronation, King Henry granted Bigod a licence to rebuild his castles at Thetford in Norfolk and Walton in Suffolk (near Felixstowe) and to build new castles at both Bungay and Framlingham in Suffolk, which were to become the Bigod family's seats of power for the next two centuries.

Roger Bigod died in September 1107 aged sixty-seven – an impressive age for those dangerous times and his body immediately became the subject of a bizarre dispute between rival clerics.

Because Roger had founded Thetford Priory, the monks there claimed the right to bury Roger's body (as well as those of his family and successors) as was the custom of the time and as had been set out in the priory's foundation charter. The monks, incidentally, were not offering to bury Roger out of the kindness of their heart but to ensure the continued financial patronage of the Bigod family. All those votive candles and chantry masses for their dead souls cost money.

Unfortunately Herbert de Losinga, the new Bishop of Norwich, argued that the body of the most important magnate in Norfolk should be buried in the new cathedral being built in the most important town in Norfolk, namely Norwich. The bishop also had ulterior motives, as he had been the Bishop of Thetford but six years previously had transferred the see (the location of the bishopric) from Thetford to Norwich and now wanted to build up the reputation of Norwich as East Anglia's ecclesiastical hub at the expense of Thetford. And, of course, having Roger buried in the new cathedral would secure the continuing patronage of the Bigod family.

In the event Bishop Losinga, another Norman who was used to getting his own way, had Roger's decomposing body stolen from Thetford Priory in the middle of the night (in a curious case of history repeating itself, while the monks were distracted celebrating matins) and, according to one version of the story, 'dragged' (presumably going bumpity-bumpity-bump against the roadway) all the way to Norwich Cathedral for reburial. The current resting place of Roger Bigod's mortal remains are unknown.

QUITE
INTRIGUING
TOO

The Death of William Rufus

Was William's death a genuine hunting accident caused by the fatal arrow deflecting off a tree? In which case why then did the alleged killer, Walter Tirel, who was known to be an excellent archer, immediately flee the country, never to return?

Or, was it an assassination engineered by William's younger brother Henry who, along with all the other courtiers who were out hunting with the king that day, including Richard de Clare and his younger brother Roger, promptly abandoned the king's body where it had fallen in the forest and galloped away to Winchester to secure the Royal Treasury and claim the throne as King Henry I. Legend has it that before setting off to go hunting on that fateful day, William said to Tirel: 'It is only right that the sharpest arrows should be given to the man who knows how to shoot the deadliest shot.'? Tirel, incidentally, was married to Richard de Clare's daughter Adelize.

Some peasants subsequently recovered the late king's corpse and carried it to Winchester, where it received a proper Christian burial although the priestly chroniclers of the time regarded William'?s death as an Act of God and a suitable end for 'a wicked king'. There again they were not entirely impartial as William and the Church had continually clashed throughout his reign and he had repeatedly appropriated ecclesiastical revenues and tithes for his own personal use.

In fact, in 1096, when the barons complained they did not have enough money to pay the latest tax he had imposed on them, William Rufus – possibly in jest – suggested they should rob the shrines of the saints. For their part, the medieval chroniclers in their monasteries did their best to blacken William's name, suggesting he was not a committed Christian and still indulged in unnatural, pagan rites.

As recently as the 1980s, the English academic and specialist in medieval history Frank Barlow described William Rufus as: 'a rumbustious, devil-may-care soldier, without natural dignity or social graces, with no cultivated tastes and little show of conventional religious piety or morality – indeed, according to his critics, addicted to every kind of vice, particularly lust and especially sodomy.' William Rufus never married.

There's a certain irony about the death of William Rufus in the New Forest, which had been set aside by his father William the Conqueror as an area of land reserved for the hunting of wild boar and deer by the royal family. (The word 'forest' is derived from Latin/Old French word *forestis* meaning a wooded area kept for hunting.) Not only was William Rufus killed there but his older brother Richard died in a hunting accident there in 1074, and three months earlier in May 1100, one of William's nephews was killed by a stray arrow.

HUGH BIGOD, THE 1ST EARL OF NORFOLK (1095-1177)

Roger Bigod was succeeded by his eldest son William Bigod, who seems to have spent a considerable amount of time at the court of Henry I. Unfortunately William was one of the approximately three hundred courtiers and sailors who drowned when the *White Ship* sank off the Normandy coast in November 1120, so he was succeeded by his younger brother Hugh.

All the leading Bigods were called either Roger or Hugh so the timeline can get confusing although you may also see this Hugh referred to as 'Hugh the Bold' and even 'Bigod the Restless' in some history books. At first he followed the family tradition of keeping in the good books of whoever was on the throne, in this case initially King Henry, with Hugh being appointed Constable of Norwich Castle in 1122 and continuing to amass property so that by the time of the King's death in 1135, he was among the ten wealthiest magnates in the country.

Then came the succession crisis. Among those to die when the *White Ship* went down was King Henry's only legitimate male heir, William Aetheling, but Henry did have a legitimate daughter Maud: known to history as the Empress Matilda through her marriage to her first husband, who had been the Holy Roman Emperor. Despite the fact

171

female rights of inheritance were unclear at this time, Henry named her as his rightful heir and successor.

This was not a popular move among the macho ranks of the Norman barons, who were all only a couple of generations away from their Viking forebears and there was an alternative candidate. This was Stephen of Blois, a nephew of King Henry and, more significantly, a grandson of William the Conqueror.

Hugh Bigod was among those courtiers in attendance when King Henry died in 1135 and it was Hugh who would later take an oath swearing that as he lay on his deathbed, the late King had changed his will and named Stephen as his heir. Evidence suggests Hugh Bigod was not even present at the time of death and a papal court subsequently ruled the oath as invalid. Nevertheless Hugh's actions helped give Stephen the legitimacy he was looking for when he effectively mounted a coup and seized the English crown.

And so began a period of English history, known as the Anarchy, a civil war that rolled backwards and forwards across the country for the better part of twenty years as supporters of King Stephen and the Empress Matilda fought for supremacy. Incidentally the *Cadfael* novels by Ellis Peters, as well as the subsequent TV series with Derek Jacobi, were set during this period.

Having been instrumental in backing Stephen, Hugh Bigod naturally pushed his luck and immediately seized Norwich Castle – only to have to reluctantly return it after Stephen pointed out it was a royal castle and that its seizure could be construed as an act of disloyalty and rebellion.

The two men patched up their differences but after Stephen was captured at the Battle of Lincoln in 1141, Hugh switched sides and became a supporter of Matilda. So grateful was Matilda (despite the fact Hugh could take a lot of the blame for starting the civil war and denying her the throne) that she conferred on him the title of Earl of Norfolk. Unfortunately Matilda began to lose her grip on the country and King Stephen escaped from captivity, with the result that Hugh found himself on the wrong side again. Soon afterwards Hugh's castle at Ipswich was seized by Stephen's forces.

At was at this point that Matilda's son, also called Henry, appeared on the scene to fight for his mother's cause and soon found that Hugh Bigod had become one of his firmest supporters. Once again fate seemed to have swung back in favour of the Bigods when, in late 1153 Stephen and Henry brokered a peace, whereby Stephen declared Henry to be his lawful successor. Just one year later Stephen fell ill with a stomach disorder and died, allowing Henry to take the throne as King Henry II rather sooner than anyone expected.

But, just as Hugh's relationship with Stephen soon soured, so things rapidly deteriorated between him and Henry II and in 1157, in an attempt to curb the power of his barons, Henry confiscated the Bigod castles, including Framlingham and Bungay, and only returned them in 1164 after the payment of a substantial fine of £666 (about £600,000 or $825,000 in today's values).

Hugh, the 1st Earl, seems to have not learned any lessons from this experience, for the following year he refused to serve the king at Norwich castle and in 1173 he was involved in a conspiracy against Henry II (known as the Great Revolt) with other barons and the king's eldest son 'Young Henry', along with the King's wife Eleanor of Aquitaine, as well as another of his sons: Richard, later to be known as King Richard the Lionheart.

Once again events initially moved in the Bigods' favour, with Hugh seizing Norwich Castle only to find, a few weeks later, that King Henry had rallied his forces and was marching through southern England and the eastern counties bringing the rebels to heel. Caught in open countryside, at Syleham in the Waveney valley, Hugh recognised his own forces were outnumbered by the royal army so rather than fight, he sued for peace and disbanded his army of Flemish mercenaries. The story is recounted in this old folk ballad:-

King Henry Marshalled His Merry Men All

Hugh Bigod was the Lord of Bungay tower,
And a merry lord was he:
So away he rode on his berry-black steed,
And sung with license and glee:

'Were I in my castle of Bungay
Upon the river of Waveney,
I would'ne give a button,
For the King of Cockney'

King Henry he marshal'd his merry men all,
And through Suffolk they march'd with speed,
And they marched to Lord Bigod's castle wall,
And knock'd at his gate, I rede

'Sir Hugh of the castle of Bungay,
upon the river of Waveney;
Come, doff your cap,
to the King of Cockney!'

Sir Hugh Bigod, so stout and brave,
in when he heard the King thus say,
He trembled and shook like a May-mawther, [young girl]
And wish'd himself away:

'Were I in my Castle on Bungay,
And beyond the River of Waveney,
I would'ne care
For the King of Cockney .'

Sir Hugh took three score sacks of gold,
And flung them over the wall;
Saying 'Go your ways, in the Devil's name,
Yourself and your merry men all!

> But leave me my castle of Bungay,
> Upon the river of Waveney,
> And I'll pay my shot,
> to the King of Cockney.'

By the summer of 1174 the rebellion was over. Hugh Bigod again kept his head but was forced to hand back Norwich Castle. In addition, four of the family's castles – Framlingham, Ipswich, Thetford and Walton – were seized by the king and demolished. The king also wanted to destroy Bungay so Hugh paid another fine (or bribe – this was the 'three score sacks of gold' mentioned in the ballad) of 1000 silver marks (about £350,000 or $480,000 at today's values) to save it from destruction.

Recognising that relations with the king were permanently poisoned, in 1176 Hugh Bigod, by then over eighty years old, set off on a pilgrimage (some reports say it was to fight in a crusade) to the Holy Land to make his peace with God. He undoubtedly needed to do this as, earlier in the reign of Henry II, he had been excommunicated by Thomas Becket, the Archbishop of Canterbury, but Hugh died (either of sickness or in a skirmish) somewhere in Syria while still on route to Jerusalem.

ROGER BIGOD, THE 2ND EARL OF NORFOLK (CIRCA 1144-1221)

Unlike his father, Roger Bigod remained loyal to Henry II during the Great Revolt (which possibly explains why his father kept his head) but as a result of a dispute with his stepmother, who challenged the Bigod inheritance on behalf of her sons by the late 1st Earl, Roger was not confirmed as the Earl of Norfolk until 1189, when Richard succeeded to the throne.

The 2nd Earl was made an ambassador to the French court, later became a *Justiciar* (in effect the realm's chief political and judicial officer, who would act as the king's deputy in England when the king was away in Europe or on a crusade) and subsequently helped negotiate and pay the ransom to secure King Richard's release from prison.

Following Richard's death in 1199, the 2ⁿᵈ Earl became an advisor to King John but this didn't stop both him and his son (Hugh Bigod, later to become the 3ʳᵈ Earl) from being among the 25 barons who acted as sureties to King John's signing of the *Magna Carta* (or Great Charter) at Runnymede in 1215 and also participated in the First Barons' War (1215–17) which followed King John's attempts to ignore the provisions of the charter he'd only just signed.

As with most of these civil wars, the picture was complicated by dynastic struggles, in this instance with Prince Louis, the son of the King of France, leading an invasion force to try to claim the English throne. Following in the family tradition, the 2ⁿᵈ Earl and his eldest son were also excommunicated for their part in forcing the King John to agree to the Magna Carta.

AND THERE WAS THE RAT IN THE SKULL

Roger Bigod was married to Ida de Tosny, who gave birth to at least six, possibly seven, children by him. However as well as being Roger's wife, she had also been one of the mistresses of Henry II and gave birth to one of his illegimate sons: William Longspée, who later became the 3ʳᵈ Earl of Salisbury. (King Henry seems to have passed Ida on the Roger after they ceased to be lovers.) William died in the year 1226 but there was a rumour he was actually murdered, by poison. Intriguingly when William's tomb was opened in 1791, the well-preserved corpse of a rat, which contained traces of arsenic, was found inside William's skull. So had the rat been poisoned and crawled away to die in William's tomb? Or had a healthy rat crawled into the tomb and eaten something it found there tainted with arsenic? I'll leave it to your own macabre imaginations to work out what it may have been.

HUGH BIGOD, THE 3ʳᵈ EARL OF NORFOLK (*CIRCA* 1182-1225)

King John died in 1217 and was succeeded by his son who ruled as King Henry III, while Prince Louis went back home to France. Roger Bigod died in 1221 and was succeeded by his son Hugh, the relatively short-lived 3ʳᵈ Earl we have already encountered at Runnymede and in the First Barons' War.

ROGER BIGOD, THE 4TH EARL OF NORFOLK (*CIRCA* 1209-70)

The eldest son of the 3rd Earl, Roger Bigod, through marriage also inherited the title of Marshall of England. By the twelfth century this was one of the highest hereditary offices within the realm and continues through to the present. Today the rank is known as the Earl Marshall and, along with organising coronations, royal funerals, and the State Opening of Parliament, also involves responsibility for running the College of Arms. Maintaining the long link with the Bigods, the current Earl Marshall is Edward Fitzalan-Howard, the 18th Duke of Norfolk.

Along with his younger brother Hugh Bigod, who as holder of the title *Justiciar* was another prominent member of the royal court, the 4th Earl was among the barons who wrested control of the government from Henry III and were allies of Simon de Montfort during the events leading up to the Second Barons' War (1264–67).

This was yet another of the civil wars that plagued England during the Middle Ages but tend to be glossed over during history lessons at school because they do get a little confusing and repetitive. As with the other rebellions of this period, this was not so much a civil war as an attempted coup and followed by multiple counter-coups by rival factions within the nobility.

The background was a long-festering enmity between Henry III and Simon de Montfort, with the latter (who was also the King's brother-in-law) wanting to reassert the *Magna Carta* and restore power to the baronial council that advised, some would say controlled the king. In 1258, a group of barons (including the Bigods) forced Henry to agree to the Provisions of Oxford, which effectively placed government in the hands of the barons, subject to a great council of nobles – called a Parliament – meeting every three years to monitor performance.

In 1261, Henry obtained a papal bull from the Pope releasing him from any obligation to honour the Provisions. Over the next couple of years both sides jockeyed for power and tried to consolidate their positions but in 1264 politics failed and fighting broke out. At the Battle of Lewes that year, the royal army was defeated and both the king and his son Edward (later King Edward I) were both captured. The following year saw the first ever English Parliament convened to meet at the Palace of Westminster (as it still does to this day) but it also saw the king's son Edward escape from captivity, rally the royalist army and fight the Battle of Evesham, where de Montfort was killed.

After this, the war began to wind down and the now effectively leaderless rebels made peace with King Henry in what is known as the Dictum of Kenilworth (not exactly a snappy title for a cause to rally round) that repudiated the Provisions of Oxford and restored royal powers. As for the Bigods? Once again they survived the strife with both their heads and their estates intact. But how did they manage this, considering both Roger and Hugh were initially supporters of Simon de Montfort?

What happened is the barons soon split between a conservative faction that supported the king, a moderate faction (which included the Bigods) who wanted some curbs on the king's powers but primarily for their own benefit, and a radical faction led by de Montfort. Given the chance, de Montfort would have made the king a mere figurehead and vested power in a Parliament that would have weakened the position of the barons by sharing their power with knights from the shires and representatives of the cities and boroughs – in other words a bunch of common oiks. (Yes, this is the origin of the House of Commons.)

Always ones to put their own interests first, the Bigods rapidly changed sides and went back to supporting the king and were in fact present on the royalist side at the Battle of Lewes. As at the Battle of Lincoln during The Anarchy, when the 1st Earl escaped from the battlefield and left his king (Stephen) to be captured, so the 4th Earl avoided capture at Lewes and abandoned his king to his fate.

ROGER BIGOD, THE 5TH EARL OF NORFOLK (*CIRCA* 1245-1306)

Roger, the 4th Earl, died childless and his estates and titles (including Marshall of England) passed to his nephew, also called Roger Bigod, who was the son of Hugh the *Justiciar*. As the 5th Earl of Norfolk, this Roger Bigod was a seemingly loyal courtier of King Edward I, acting on his behalf in both Wales and Ireland although he earns his place in the history books for an argument he had with Edward in 1297.

King Edward had ordered Bigod to lead an army against the King of France in Gascony, while Edward led another force in Flanders. Bigod refused, claiming that by the feudal tenure of his lands he was only compelled to serve across the seas 'in the company of the king himself'.

This prompted Edward to say: 'By God, Sir Earl, you shall either go or hang.'

To which Bigod replied: 'By the same oath, O King, I will neither go nor hang.'

The 5th Earl did not go to France, nor did he hang. In fact after Edward had departed for France, Roger Bigod, along with Humphrey de Bohun, the Earl of Hereford (and also Constable of England) plus a number of other barons and the Archbishop of Canterbury drew up an official complaint (called The Remonstrances – another snappy title) and prevented the collection of taxes to support the war effort. As Edward was simultaneously fighting wars in Wales, Scotland and France at this time and the barons were feeling the pinch, to the point where the country seemed on the brink of another civil war.

In the event, military setbacks in Scotland forced King Edward to negotiate a truce with the French and make peace with his barons, with Edward confirming (in another memorably titled document called the *Confirmatio Cartarum*) his compliance with *Magna Carta* and other royal charters that protected the feudal rights of the barons.

The nineteenth century historian William Stubbs subsequently described Bigod and his ally Humphrey de Bohun as 'but degenerate sons of mighty fathers, greater in their opportunities than in their patriotism,' although the evidence of the previous two centuries suggests the Bigods were always opportunists and Roger's actions very much followed the family tradition.

Edward was to have the last laugh in 1302 when the elderly, childless and deeply in debt the 5th Earl was forced to negotiate a deal with the king whereby he made Edward his heir and in return received a generous pension on which to live out his days. Technically Roger surrendered his title and received it back entailed 'to the heirs of his body'. This meant when he died in December 1306, his title could not be passed to his brother's family (as previous earls had done) but became extinct with the result all the Bigod estates, including their castles, were transferred to the Crown.

There is an additional irony here in that for many years Roger had only been kept solvent by borrowing money from members of the Jewish community who, at the time, were the only people in England permitted to lend money, and were barred from many other lines of work. In 1290, having exploited them to the point where they were no longer of financial use to the crown, Edward expelled all the Jews from England and promptly cut off the major source of credit for the Bigods and many of the other barons.

King Edward himself died in 1307 and his son Edward II bestowed the title of Earl of Norfolk and all the Bigod estates on Thomas of Brotherton, his half-brother (the eldest son from Edward I's second marriage). And so the great dynasty of the Bigods, the king-makers who had dominated East Anglia since the Norman Conquest over two centuries earlier, ended with not so much a bang as a whimper.

THE LAST OF THE BIGODS

After the Bigod Earls of Norfolk had shuffled off the stage, we hear no more about the Bigods in the history books until January 1537 when a certain Sir Francis Bigod, a descendant of the Bigod earls launched an under-resourced and poorly thought-through rebellion in Yorkshire against Henry VIII's religious reforms. Bigod seems to have been inspired by the previous year's Pilgrimage of Grace. This was a protest by Roman Catholics, also mainly in Yorkshire, against Henry's Protestant reforms, particularly the Dissolution of the Monasteries, and was notable for the lenient treatment of the rebels, who were all pardoned amid promises that the fate of the abbeys would be reviewed by Parliament.

Unfortunately Bigod's rebellion merely convinced King Henry and his advisors (who included Sir Thomas Howard, the 3rd Duke of Norfolk, another family following the Bigods as the premier peers in Norfolk) that Catholics could not be trusted. The result was not only did Sir Francis end his days at Tyburn on the end of a rope (although in not quite such a dramatic fashion as poor Brother Essric at St Benet's some five hundred years earlier) but the king also used this as an excuse to round up all the previously-pardoned leaders of the Pilgrimage of Grace and have 216 of them found guilty of treason. They were all duly executed by being 'hung, drawn, disembowelled and quartered', beheaded, just plain hanged or, in the case of poor Lady Margaret Cheney – 'a very fair creature and beautiful' – burned at the stake in Smithfield.

THE BIGOD CASTLES

Today, the remaining parts of the Bigod's **Bungay Castle** amount to little more than a few stretches of the curtain walls and the ruins of the gatehouse towers yet from just this, it is still possible to picture the scale of the castle in its heyday, dominating not just the town of Bungay but the whole of the Waveney valley from its position on high ground above a river that protects it on three sides.

Subsequent excavations and reconstructions suggest that at its peak, the castle had walls nearly 25 feet thick and a keep 110 feet high. If you stand at the top of the tower of the nearby church of St Mary's (the tower is open from time-to-time to the public) you will be at approximately the same height as a man-at-arms standing guard on the battlements of Bungay Castle's keep in its heyday.

Ironically, in terms of its history the castle proved to be anything but impregnable. Built in around 1100 by the first Roger Bigod, Henry II confiscated it from Hugh, the 1st Earl in 1157 and only returned it in

1164 after Hugh had paid a substantial fine. Well, perhaps not that substantial as the following year Hugh built a new keep and reinforced the site. Ten years later Hugh found himself on the losing side in the Great Revolt and in its course Henry's forces mined Bungay Castle in an attempt to destroy it. Mining a castle involved digging a tunnel under the walls and then lighting a bonfire, fuelled by pig fat, which would cause the tunnel to collapse and bring down part of the walls.

Henry paid an even bigger fine to save the castle, which was subsequently returned to the Bigods. The next three earls had little to do with Bungay and it was left to the 5th Earl to complete the final building phase of renovating the castle and erecting the gatehouse towers (at the time the second largest gatehouse in England) in 1294, a project which, ironically, only contributed to his own personal financial ruin. When he died, ownership of the castle reverted to the crown. After this, the castle rapidly fell into disrepair and by as early as 1382 it was described as being 'old and ruinous and worth nothing a year'.

One hundred years later, in 1483, the castle was given to the Howard family Dukes of Norfolk, who continued to own the increasingly decrepit ruins until 1987, when the 17th Duke of Norfolk presented the deeds to the castle to the town of Bungay. It is now administered and repaired by the town's castle trust.

In the intervening five centuries between 1483 and 1987 the castle was sold and bought back by the Dukes of Norfolk on several occasions. A builder owned it in 1766 – he planned to demolish it and use the rubble for roadmaking. In 1792 a local solicitor, Daniel Bonhote, bought it for his wife Elizabeth. She had a house built between the two gatehouse towers and wrote her Gothic romance *Bungay Castle* there. Next we hear of it being owned by a local branch of the Oddfellows, who built a meeting hall there, but they sold it back to the Duke for £6,000 in 1898.

The early history of **Framlingham Castle** is far from clear. There may have been a Saxon high status building on the site before the Norman

Conquest, which was built over by the first Roger Bigod in around 1100. This castle was either reinforced or demolished and rebuilt by Hugh, the 1st Earl, during The Anarchy, but subsequently destroyed on the orders of Henry II in the aftermath of the defeat of the Great Revolt. There's an archive record of the King's Engineer submitting an account showing that £16 pounds 11 shillings and 2 pence were spent on the castle's destruction.

Hugh's son Roger, the 2nd Earl, was granted permission by King Richard to rebuild the castle. This was completed by 1213 and featured the novel design of large walled inner courtyard surrounded by thirteen mural towers. Three years later the castle was surrounded by the forces of King John during the First Barons' War and, mindful of the recent fate of Rochester Castle in Kent, which was successfully mined by the royal army, Roger Bigod negotiated the surrender of the castle without a fight.

Once again the Bigods' luck held and in 1225 we hear of Roger's grandson, the 4th Earl, living at Framlingham. In the years that followed, the Bigods began building deer parks, lakes and pleasure gardens at Framlingham, as it slowly mutated from a fortress into a more luxurious residence. All this came to an end when the 5th Earl died and the castle reverted to the Crown.

In the years that followed, it was given to successive generations of the earls and, later, dukes of Norfolk, including the Brothertons, the Uffords, the Mowbrays and finally the Howards. Sometimes the castle was the focal point of the earls' and dukes' households and social activities. For example, in 1385 there 83 people living there, spending £1,000 a year on the purchase of 28,567 imperial gallons of ale and 70,321 loaves of bread. But at other times the castle was ignored.

Major repairs and renovations were made by the Howards during the Tudor period – that is, when the Howards were not being carted off to the Tower of London accused of treason and losing their properties and/or their heads. By my reckoning, during the period 1400 to 1600, five Dukes of Norfolk spent time imprisoned in the

Tower of London, with one dying there, another exiled, another released but subsequently killed in battle, and two executed for high treason.

The castle's last hurrah was in 1553 when Mary Tudor made Framlingham her base before setting off for London to claim the throne as Queen Mary I.

After Mary, the decline was rapid and by 1589 a survey noted that the stonework, timber and brickwork all needed urgent maintenance. By then, the castle was being used as a royal prison – primarily for Catholic priests although legend has it the castle was in such poor repair that the priests had to find lodgings in a nearby village. Two changes of ownership later it was in the hands of Pembroke College, Cambridge, and for the next two hundred years was the site of the county poorhouse.

When the poorhouse became redundant, being replaced by a new workhouse at Wickham Market, the castle was used for a variety purposes, including serving as a county court before being donated to the Commissioner of Works in 1913 for preservation as an ancient monument. Today it is owned by English Heritage and run as a tourist attraction, incorporating a local history museum, as well as a shop and café. But you can't buy ale by the gallon any more.

At one point **Ipswich Castle**, which was built after the Norman Conquest, fell into the hands of Hugh Bigod, the 1st Earl. But after Henry II defeated the Great Revolt, he punished the rebel barons by destroying their fortresses and in the case of the Bigods, this meant the destruction of Ipswich Castle. In sharp contrast with the fate of Norwich, the castle at Ipswich was never rebuilt and nothing remains of it today. Even its exact location (as well as its construction and layout) is a mystery.

Thetford Castle was Roger Bigod's original seat of power and in 1100 he was given permission to replace the old Norman Conquest-era castle with a new motte-and-bailey castle comprising a huge artificial mound (the motte) surrounded by a deep surrounding ditch and earthwork ramparts. The motte was topped by a large timber keep with a timber-walled (later replaced by stone) bailey (enclosed courtyard) completing the fortifications.

During the struggles between the 1st Earl and Henry II, Thetford Castle was seized by the King in 1157 but then was recaptured by the Bigods in 1173. In the aftermath of the rebels' defeat, Henry also had this castle destroyed but the earthworks (the motte is over sixty feet and reckoned to be the second largest man-made mound in England – the largest is Silbury Hill in Wiltshire) proved indestructible and today form part of the municipal Castle Park.

Legend has it that six solid silver bells from Thetford Priory are buried at the base of the mound. They are not, so please do not go digging around for them! (Or 'No diggin' 'ere!' as William Agers, the guardian of buried treasure, would say in M.R. James' supernatural horror tale *A Warning to the Curious*.)

The least known of the Bigod fortresses is **Walton Castle**, which is said to have been located on cliffs nearly ninety feet above sea level near what is now the coastal town of Felixstowe. Walton is the most ancient of all the Bigod castles, having originally been built by the Romans in the third century as part of their Saxon Shore defences. Later it became the site of a Saxon church (and possibly the site of Dommoc where St Felix established his bishopric) and was then refortified by Roger Bigod, who used the original Roman walls to create a bailey.

In the aftermath of the 1173 revolt, Henry II also confiscated and dismantled Walton Castle, using the stone to help construct Orford Castle. While some of the flint and brick walls of the Roman fort survived, these were largely destroyed by coastal erosion during the eighteenth century, although the last remnants of wall can apparently still be seen from the beach during exceptionally low tides.

Finally, despite the fact the Bigods, particularly Hugh, the 1st Earl, spent much of their time plotting to get their hands on **Norwich Castle**, it remained a royal stronghold throughout the Norman and Plantagenet eras. In fact until Orford Castle was built by Henry II – primarily as a check on the power of the Bigods – Norwich was the only major royal castle in East Anglia. By 1345, the castle had become the county gaol, a role it continued to have until 1887, when it was bought by the City of Norwich and converted into a museum. Today it remains open to the public as a museum and art gallery.

Appendix 3

An Alternative History of how Britain was Colonised

In early 2014 it was announced that following scientific analysis, a set of fossilised hominin footprints discovered in May 2013, in a newly uncovered sediment layer on a beach at Happisburgh in Norfolk, had been dated to the early Pleistocene Age. This is over 800,000 years ago, making them the oldest known hominin footprints outside of Africa.

The hominins who left these footprints were a very early archaic ancestor of modern humans, pre-dating even Neanderthals by 400,000 years. The same Ancient Human Occupation of Britain Project team also found a number of worked flints at Pakefield, which is about twenty miles south of Happisburgh on the Norfolk coast – and just eight miles from Hopton-on-Sea – which have been dated to around 700,000 years ago.

In other words people, albeit very primitive people, have been living at what is now the eastern end of the Waveney valley for nearly one million years. The story is not one of continuous occupation as we also know that, thanks to the Ice Ages, the local climate would have varied dramatically between polar conditions and temperatures more like the modern Mediterranean. The result was any people living in the British Isles would have only been temporary occupants before being driven out by successive Ice Ages.

This process was repeated perhaps eight or nine times, maybe even more, before the last ice-sheet receded some 12,500 years ago. Only then, were a fresh wave of migrants able to cross the land-bridge from Europe and permanently re-colonise British Isles. Many of us reading this book are their direct descendants. Well that is the

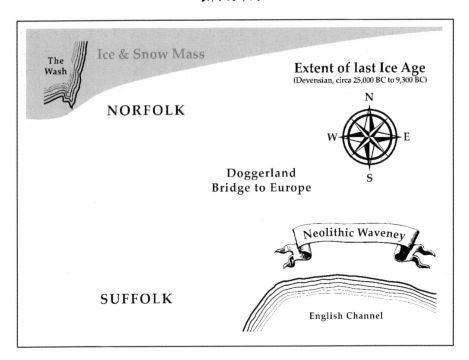

scientific explanation of how the British Isles were colonised but legend and myth offer an alternative explanation.

TALES OF BRAVE BRUTUS AND EVIL GOGMAGOG

According to classical Greek and Roman writers of the period 300 BC to AD 400, the word Britannia referred to the entire British Isles and comprised two main islands: Albion (encompassing England, Wales and Scotland) and Ierné or Hibernia (Ireland).

As to the origins of the name Albion, according to the story first set out by the notoriously fanciful twelfth century historian Geoffrey of Monmouth* in his *History of the Kings of Britain* and subsequently expanded in an early fourteenth century Anglo-Norman poem called *Brut* the name is derived from a princess called Albina.

> * Geoffrey of Monmouth's near contemporary, the
> chronicler William of Newburgh once commented: 'It is
> quite clear that everything this man wrote [about the early
> Kings of Britain] was made up.'

The way the legend tells it, a certain king of Greece (or it may have been Syria) had thirty daughters (or it may have been thirty-three – there are several versions of this story) and married them off into other royal families. These daughters were exceedingly haughty and unwilling to be subservient to their new husbands, so they plotted to kill them. Sadly for them, news of the plot leaked out, so their father ordered the thirty princesses to be put aboard an unsteerable, rudderless ship and set adrift.

If folklore tales are any measure, casting people adrift in a rudderless boat and leaving them to their fate seems to have been a popular method of disposing of royal criminals in ancient times. In most instances it would have been a death sentence but it left the authorities without blood on their hands and able to attribute the condemned's death to divine judgement.

After many days at sea, the boat washed up on the shore of unknown and uninhabited island. The eldest daughter, Albina, was the first to set foot on the shore and lay claim to the land, naming it after herself. In the weeks that followed, the women learned to hunt animals but apparently eating meat 'aroused their lecherous desires' and they began to have sexual relations with demons and evil spirits. The offspring of these relationships was a race of giants. Readers may note this is very similar to the Old Testament tale of the Fallen Angels taking human women as wives and them giving birth to a race of giants called the Nephilim.

Some 260 years later, according to the legend, a boat containing an exiled Trojan warrior called Brutus and his band of followers arrived on the island of Albion. They found the island's only inhabitants were twenty-four giants – the sole remaining descendants of Albina and her sisters' paranormal hanky-panky. The Trojans killed all the giants except their leader Gogmagog. He wrestled with Brutus' companion Corineus, who killed the giant by throwing him off a cliff.

Brutus then became the king of Albion, renaming it Britonum after himself and establishing his capital in London, while Corineus became the ruler of the south-western corner of the island, which was renamed Cornwall in his honour.

The battle between Gogmagog and Corineus is said to have taken place on Plymouth Ho! and for several hundred years, until it was destroyed by the construction of a new fort in the 1660s, the outline of two giants were cut into the white chalk of the Hoe.

Later, Gogmagog and Corineus also became the unofficial guardians of the City of London, with the two statues depicting them decorating the interior of the Guildhall since at least the 1550s. We are actually now on the third pair of statues: the originals were destroyed in the Great Fire of London in 1666, their replacements were bombed during the Blitz in 1940, and the new pair date from 1953. Also, somewhere along the way poor Corineus was forgotten and the two statues are now known as Gog and Magog.

The story of Brutus and his companions killing the giants, who originally occupied Albion, does raise the intriguing possibility this legend has roots spreading far, far back into prehistory to a time when early modern humans (that is the *Homo sapiens* who are our direct ancestors) encountered the older, stockier Neanderthal branch of the human family tree. Certainly the two species coexisted in Europe for many thousands of years.

QUITE INTRIGUING TOO

The Woodwose

While we are all familiar with the idea of some kind of missing-link, primitive human-like creatures still living in the Himalayas (the Yeti a.k.a. the Abominable Snowman) and in the forests of the American North-West (the Sasquatch a.k.a. Bigfoot), we need recall that throughout the medieval period there were rumours of comparable wildmen living in the forests of Europe – and England.

Called the Woodwose (or Wodewose – from the Anglo-Saxon *Wuduwasa*) they were said to be human-like except their bodies were covered in thick hair. Theories as to their origin vary from them being dispossessed peoples driven out to live in the forests and wild places by later invaders, through to their being late surviving communities of Neanderthals. Whatever they were, they made a sufficient impact upon the medieval mindset that wildmen are regularly depicted in European heraldry on coats-of-arms, typically depicted as bearded, naked men (which just a wreath of leaves on

The Cratfield Woodwose.
Photo: Charles Christian.

Saxmundum woodwose. Photo: David Taylor.

their heads and another wreath around their middles to protect their dignity) wielding large wooden clubs.

Curiously the woodwose/wildman is also a popular ornamentation, either above doorways on porches or as supports for baptism fonts in medieval churches across Norfolk and Suffolk. (All the locations are either too far to the south or to the north to be legimately included in this book.) In Suffolk there are particularly fine examples at St Mary's Chediston, St Peter's Sibton and St John the Baptist, Saxmundham, the latter complete with a contemporary fifteenth century flat cap. St Mary's Cratfield depicts a very hairy woodwose on the front porch about to do battle with a wyvern, as does a similar pair of carvings at St Michael's Peasenhall.

In Norfolk you can find woodwoses at, among other places, on the misericordia at Norwich Cathedral, St Catherine's Ludham, St Mary's Happisburgh, St Edmunds Acle, St Margaret's Hapton, and St Nicholas North Walsham. But best not mention St Nicholas at

Potter Heigham where a woodwose stands in a niche above the entrance – rumour has it the carving was found buried in the churchyard and placed in the niche in the mistaken belief it depicted St Nicholas.

Are woodwoses just a medieval remembrance of even earlier wildmen (and women) who long ago lived on the margins of civilisation? Perhaps not as there have been numerous reports in recent years of wild men or 'British Bigfoots' being sighted across the UK. These include 'The Beast of the A1075' which apparently lurks on a road passing through Thetford Forest in the Brecklands area of Norfolk. This has been spotted in 1986, 2007 and 2009, with possible related sightings in 1979, 2011 and 2017.

Best be on your guard: one legend says woodwose will eat children!

AND WAS DOGGERLAND ATLANTIS?

While there is no disputing the now sunken landmass in the middle of the North Sea played an invaluable role in the post-Ice Age repopulation of the British Isles, one of the more fantastic myths associated with Doggerland is it was actually the location of the fabled lost civilisation of Atlantis.

There are of course numerous locations identified as the possible site of Atlantis. These include: beyond the Pillars of Hercules in the mid-Atlantic, somewhere near the present day Azores. The Black Sea, which some writers claim was the site of a deluge that gave rise to the story of the Great Flood of Genesis, Noah and his Ark. The island of Santorini in the Mediterranean, where the eruption of the volcano Thera sometime around 1,600 to 1,500 BC may have caused the collapse of the Minoan civilisation. The Baltic Sea and even the Scilly Isles and the lost Kingdom of Lyonesse at the western end of the St Michael and St Mary Alignment. (One of the reasons why this alignment is sometimes also referred to as the Atlantis ley-line.)

Returning to Doggerland, its claim to be the location of a lost civilisation can be traced back to the middle of the nineteenth century when what purported to be an ancient manuscript, apparently handwritten in the Old Frisian language, was submitted for publication. It was subsequently translated and published in Dutch and English in the mid-1870s and immediately became the subject of heated controversy.

Called the *Oera Linda Book* (or *Thet Oera Linda Bok* in Frisian) it purported to be a chronicle of historical, mythological and religious themes from around 2,000 BC to the thirteenth century AD. It began with an account of the island of Atland (or Adland or the Old Land/Home Country) located in the North Sea, being lost beneath the sea in a cataclysm in 2,194 BC. According to the book's authors this was the same date as Noah's Flood in the Bible.

Its people then settled on the North Sea coast of the Netherlands and Denmark, where they worshipped the goddess Freyja (or Freya – the area is today known as Frisia and takes its name from the goddess) and were ruled by a kindly matriarchy of folk-mothers until their beliefs were crushed by callous Christian missionaries.

The book went on to claim the people of Atland and, later, Frisia, developed a major maritime culture, founding the city of Tyre in the Lebanon, and even establishing the Inca empire in South America. It also claimed the Frisian civilisation possessed an alphabet that was the ancestor of the Greek and Phoenician alphabets.

Soon after its publication there were claims that it was a fake and by 1880 it was widely recognised as a hoax by academics. It was then forgotten for over fifty years until it was rediscovered by a *volkisch* philologist called Herman Wirth who, in 1933, published a German translation, which he described it as a Nordic Bible. (The nearest English equivalent of *volkisch* is ethno-nationalistic folklore, which nowadays has racist connotations)

The book was popular with a senior member of the German Nazi Party, Heinrich Himmler, who was obsessed with Aryan mysticism, and it soon became associated with Nazi occultism. But at a conference at the University of Berlin in 1934, the book was once more condemned as a satirical hoax and a forgery and fell out of favour for another fortyy-five years until it was taken up by the Englishman Robert J..Scrutton in his books *The Other Atlantis* and *Secrets of Lost Atland*. Since then the *Oera Linda Book*, at least in

England, has become associated with Earth mysteries, alternative history and other New Age beliefs including, more recently, neopaganism and witchcraft. But is it a hoax? Is it a historical forgery? The answer to both questions is yes.

The historical evidence is stacked against Doggerland ever having been home to an advanced civilisation. Archaeological findings (including animal remains, human remains, worked flints, harpoons delicately crafted from antlers and, most recently, a carved and decorated piece of bison bone dating back 13,500 years) have been dredged from the Doggerland site between East Anglia and the Dutch coast but they are only consistent with a hunter-gatherer culture of the Mesolithic-Neolithic period. And, as already mentioned, Doggerland vanished sometime around 5,000 BC, which is about 3,000 years earlier than the 2,194 BC date given in the *Oera Linda Book*.

The book also contains a number of anachronisms, which suggest a mid-nineteenth century rather than thirteenth century or earlier authorship. Plus, the fact that even the Nazis rejected the book as a fraud should be damning enough. Afterall the Nazis had plenty of crazy crackpot beliefs of their own about Nordic supermen living within a hollow Earth accessed by flying saucers through secret tunnels linking the North and South Poles, and if they thought it was a hoax…

So to who actually wrote it and why?

The Professor of Frisian Language and Literature Goffe Jensma wrote in 2004 that the most likely candidates were three nineteenth century writers: Cornelis Over de Linden (the man who originally 'found' the manuscript and submitted it for publication), Eelco Verwijs, and Pastor Francois Haverschmidt. Jensma posits it was intended 'to be a temporary hoax to fool some nationalist Frisians and orthodox Christians and as an exercise in reading the Holy Bible in a non-fundamentalist, symbolical way…' Jensma has also noted that: 'It is a perfect irony that a book written to unmask the Holy Bible as a book of human making was itself to become treated as gospel.'

Poe's Law

The *Oera Linda Book* is a classic example of what in the current Digital Age would be called Poe's Law. This takes its name from Nathan (not Edgar Allen) Poe who coined it in 2005 on an internet forum on religion. Poe said that without a clear indicator of the author's intent – such as a winking smiley or other blatant display of humour – it is impossible to create a parody of extreme views so obviously exaggerated that it would not be taken seriously by some readers for a sincere expression of the views being parodied.

Further Reading and Resources

Hugh Aldersey-Williams, *The Adventures of Sir Thomas Browne in the 21st Century*, Granta Books, 2016

Jason R. Ali, 'The orientation of churches: Some new evidence' *The Antiquaries Journal*, December 2001

Frank Barlow, *William Rufus*, University of California Press, 1983

Bede, *The Ecclesiastical History of the English People*

Elizabeth Bonhote, *Bungay Castle*, 1796

Janet and Colin Bord, *Atlas of Magical Britain*, Sidgwick & Jackson, 1990

Brian Branston, *The Lost Gods of England*, Thames and Hudson, 1974

Pamela Brooks, *Suffolk Ghosts and Legends*, Halsgrove, 2009

Julius Caesar, *Commentaries on the Gallic War (Comentarii de Bello Gallico)*

Robert Chambers, *The Book of Days, A Miscellany of Popular Antiquities*, W. & R. Chambers, 1888

Cormac Mac Cuilennain, *Sanas Cormaic*

Daniel Defoe, *A Tour of the Whole Island of Great Britain*, 1724–7

Clive Dunn, *Landscape of Towers*, Lasse Press, 2019

H.P.R. Finberg, *The Formation of England 550–1042*, Paladin, 1976

Abraham Fleming, *A Strange & Terrible Wunder, Wrought Very Late in the Parish of Bongay (in 1577)*, reprinted Ulan Press, 2012

James George Frazer, *The Golden Bough: A Study in Magic and Religion*, reprinted Dover Publications, 2003

Carolyne Larrington, *The Land of the Green Man*, I.B. Tauris, 2017

Geofrey of Monmouth, *Historia Regum Britanniae*, 1136

M.J. Harper and H.L. Vered, *The Megalithic Empire,* Nathan Carmody, 2012

Holinshed's Chronicles, 1587

Basil Harold, *An Enigma of Ancient Suffolk, South Elmham Before 1066*, Red Bird Press, 2003

M.R. James, 'The Ash-tree' *Ghost Stories of an Antiquary*, 1904

M.R. James, 'The Mezzotint' *Ghost Stories of an Antiquary*, 1904

M.R. James, 'The Stalls of Barchester Cathedral' *More Ghost Stories of an Antiquary*, 1911

M.R. James, *The Wanderings and Homes of Manuscripts*, S.P.C.K., 1919

M.R. James, 'A Warning to the Curious' *A Warning to the Curious and Other Ghost Stories*, 1925

M.R. James, *Suffolk and Norfolk*, J.M. Dent, 1930

Goffe Jensma, 'How to Deal with Holy Books in an Age of Emerging Science. The Oera Linda Book as a New Age Bible' *Fabula 48*, November 2007

Carenza Lewis, ' Disaster recovery? New archaeological evidence from eastern England for the impact of the 'calamitous' 14th century' *Antiquity* vol. 90, 2016

Clements Markham, 'Pytheas the Discoverer of Britain' *The Geographical Journal*, June 1893

Arthur Mee, *The King's England: Norfolk*, Hodder and Stoughton, 1940

Arthur Mee, *The King's England: Suffolk*, Hodder and Stoughton, 1941

John Michell, *The New View Over Atlantis*, Thames and Hudson, 1983

Eric Pursehouse, *Waveney Valley Studies*, Diss Publishing, 1966

Nikolaus Pevsner, *The Buildings of England: Suffolk* (Second Edition), Penguin, 1974

Christopher Reeve, *Paranormal Suffolk*, Amberley, 2009

Lillias Rider Haggard (editor), *I Walked by Night – Being the Life & History of the King of the Norfolk Poachers, Written by Himself*, Ivor Nicholson and Watson, 1935

Reader's Digest, *Folklore Myths and Legends of Britain*, Reader's Digest, 1973

Charles Sampson, *Ghosts of the Broads*, Jarrold Colour Publications, 1976 edition

Robert J Scrutton, *Secrets of Lost Atland*, TBS, 1978

Robert J Scrutton, *The Other Atlantis*, Sphere, 1979

Grant and Jane Solomon, *The Scole Experiment: Scientific Evidence for Life After Death*, Campion Books, 2006 revised edition

F.M. Stenton, *Anglo-Saxon England*, Oxford 1970

Alfred Suckling, *The Histories and Antiquities of Suffolk*, 1846

Ernest R. Suffing, *The Land of the Broads*, Upcott Gill, 1887

Danny Sullivan, *Ley Lines: A Comprehensive Guide to Alignments*, Piatkus, 1999

Peter Tolhurst, *This Hollow Land: Aspects of Norfolk Folklore*, Black Dog Books, 2018

Alfred Watkins, *The Old Straight Track*, Heritage Hunter, 2015 edition

Martin Welch, *Anglo-Saxon England*, Batsford, 1992

Michael Wood, *In Search of the Dark Ages*, BBC, 1981

Jennifer Westwood and Jacqueline Simpson, *The Lore of the Land*, Penguin Books, 2005

WEBSITES

Ancient Origins: www.ancient-origins.net

Convict Records: https://convictrecords.com.au

Folklore Society: https://folklore-society.com

Hidden East Anglia: www.hiddenea.com

Paranormal Database: www.paranormaldatabase.com

St Michael and St Mary Ley-Line on Google Maps:
www.google.com/maps/d/viewer?mid=1EfTggFzl0UQ1W_Ls45
K2Cl_H6eE&hl=en_US&ll=52.319259934691765%2C1.216065
588409947&z=11

MAPS

Ordnance Survey Explorer 230: Diss & Harleston

Ordnance Survey Explorer 231: Southwold & Bungay

Ordnance Survey Explorer OL 40: The Broads